SUNG AC~~ROSS~~
HEROIC POETRY OF ILLYRIA

MUNDUS ARTIUM PRESS

English language translation copyright © 2011 by
Mundus Artium Press
All rights reserved
Manufactured in the United States of America

04   21   11   -   0   2   +

No part of this book may be reproduced or utilized in any form or by any means, electronic or mechanical, including photocopying, recording, or by any information storage or retrieval system, without permission in writing from the Publisher. Inquiries should be addressed to Permissions Department:

MUNDUS ARTIUM PRESS
The University of Texas at Dallas
Center for Translation Studies,
800 West Campbell Road, JO51
Richardson, TX 75080-3021

Library of Congress Cataloging-in-Publication Data

Mundus Artium Press; 2011 /
Sung Across the Shoulder: Heroic Poetry of Illyria / translated by Gjekë Marinaj and Frederick Turner /
ISBN 978-0-939378-11-1 (pbk.) I. Title.

Cover image: "Home Again" (2006) by Gjekë Marinaj
Marinaj Photograph: "Marinaj, 2010" By Jesse Bowen
Turner Photograph: By TSHIND Photos

Published by:

MUNDUS ARTIUM PRESS
The University of Texas at Dallas
Center for Translation Studies,
800 West Campbell Road, JO51
Richardson, TX 75080-3021

ISBN 978-0-939378-11-1

SUNG ACROSS THE SHOULDER:
HEROIC POETRY OF ILLYRIA

Translated, edited, and introduced by
GJEKË MARINAJ and FREDERICK TURNER

MUNDUS ARTIUM PRESS

CONTENTS

5

FOREWORD

DEAD OR ALIVE: TRANSLATING THE VIOLENT BEAUTY OF ALBANIAN FOLK POETRY

By Frederick TURNER

> *Manuel Torres, a man with more culture in his veins than anybody I have known, when listening to Falla play his own "Nocturno del Genaralife," made his splendid pronouncement: "All that has dark sounds has duende."And there is no greater truth.*
>
> *These dark sounds are the mystery, the roots thrusting into the fertile loam known to all of us, ignored by all of us, but from which we get what is real in art...*
>
> *Thus duende is a power and not a behavior, it is a struggle and not a concept. I have heard an old master guitarist say: "Duende is not in the throat; duende surges up from the soles of the feet." Which means it is not a matter of ability, but of real live form; of blood; of ancient culture; of creative action.*
>
> --Federico Garcia Lorca: "Duende: Theory and Divertissement," composed and delivered by Lorca during his stay in Havana en route from the United States; subsequently repeated in Buenos Aires for the Sociedad Amigos del Arte (1934)

That dark sound is familiar in the great folk poetries of the world: we hear it in the bitter love songs of the Auvergne, in the Scots border ballads, in the Blues, in the Tang ballads of the old Chinese frontier, in the gests of the Greek pallikares and the piney-woods of Appalachia.

It comes to us with special force in the folk poetry of Albania, which I and my colleague, the distinguished Albanian poet Gjekë Marinaj, have been translating for the last few years.

9

Though the fatal starkness and unrestrained but understated passion of this poetry is in some ways universal to folk traditions all over the globe, there are unique elements in the Albanian legacy, a going to extremes that is exceptional and that in some ways defines the outer limit of the human popular imagination. There is also a wider range of genres than is usual, perhaps due to the great antiquity of Balkan mountain culture.

To the north and east of Tirana lie spectacular ranges of mountains, extending into Kosovo and Macedonia, where fierce independent shepherd peoples have lived for millennia, speaking one of the oldest dialects of the great Indo-European language group. They have been invaded many times, by Italians, Greeks, and especially Turks, who occupied their lands for centuries, but they never lost their language or culture. The writ of the invaders seldom ran far from the coast and the plains, and the mountain people kept their pride, their women, their poetry, and their weapons. As Noc Mark Deda says in "Word Spreads in Istanbul":

> "I'll not give up my guns alive,
> My guns I'll not give up alive!
> I'll wash the dales in blood that day
> They come to take my guns away."

Albanians are divided between those who converted to Islam and those who kept their Christian (Catholic or Orthodox) traditions despite economic oppression. But whatever side of the great battle of Kosovo (1389) they would have supported, the poetry of the mountain people is proudly independent, and celebrates the values of a patriarchal society — male and female honor, piety, local pride, Albanian patriotism, a passionate love of the land and the herder's life, and the vendetta. The flavor

10

of their ferocious love of their land is nicely caught in "Homage to the Warriors":

HOMAGE TO THE WARRIORS

When I take my lute to sing
Snow-peaks perch upon my string,
And the forest heights fall still
And the starry heavens chill
And the ice-fields and the crests
Come to sing the heroes' gests.
Words like water from the spring
Teach the heroes' deeds to sing;
Green-clad hillsides raise the call
Echoed from the mountain-wall.

Time harrows rocks and stones and all,
Yet heroes for the flag still fall;
The Cemi brook runs red with gore,
But their mothers will bear more.
They give birth to bravery,
Let the Alban eagles fly.

Before we go any further with this introduction, something needs to be said about the poems in this collection. Most of them have never been in print — certainly not in these particular versions, and never before in English. Later I will say something about our translation methods, but the immediate point here is that these poems, like the lives of the people they record, are things of breath and memory, as vulnerable to time and death and forgetfulness as the heartbeat itself, and the more vivid and committed for that very fact. Are we rendering them less valid by preserving them in print and on memory disks?

At the heart of the Albanian oral poet's love of his land is the daily and authentic sweetness of the shepherd's life. From "Songs of the Dairy" we get vivid little rhythmic pictures of that life, as in this piece:

BUTTER

> Churn, churn, churnabumble,
> Pour the milk and hear it tumble,
> Churn, churn, churnabumble,
> Sweetly let the plunger rumble.
> Churn, churn, churnabumble,
> Winking eyeballs from the mold,
> Churn, churn, churnabumble,
> Secret to the shepherd told,
> Churn, churn, churnabumble:
> Butter is the shepherd's gold.

The poets are convinced of the superiority of their way of life in point of health, vigor, and moral force. In the delightful poem "In the Mountains of Taramis," which combines a lyrical appreciation of the landscape with comic satire on urban decadence, the poet contrasts the mustachioed and terrifying young men of the mountains with the lesser men of the plains:

> In the mountains where it snows
> No doctor needs to show his nose,
> Apothecaries we don't need,
> No medicines at all, indeed:
> Where at noon the sun won't burn,
> Where winds dance with the waving fern,

Where the grasses sweetly sing,
Strawberries ripen in the spring,
Where the shepherd's song is merry,
Drinking milk with sweet strawberry
Iced with snow and berry-fresh,
That renews an old man's flesh,
Turns an old man to a young,
Makes his feet so swift and strong,
He climbs mountains all day long.
...
Of city people I might tell,
But they self-advertise too well.
They eat less, it is very true,
But they have so much less to do.
They are so scared that they will die,
They live where doctors are nearby.
No young man here is such a chump,
He knows a good place from a dump,
Summers he hikes up in the hills,
Comes down in winter from the chills,
That's why our youth is strong and hale,
Not short and skinny, thin and frail;
They do not lack mustache or beard,
And their looks are justly feared,
They make you feel a feeble beast—
They don't need money in the least!

This last line implies ominously that the young men of Malësisë
don't need to buy things—they can take what they want, or
rather, people will supply it out of fear before the big fellow
puts his hand in his pocket. But the line also means that the
mountain men are off the grid of the money economy—they

live in the ancient heroic world of gifts and tribute.

This life is one in which women are valuable property, like Helen of Troy, not to be stolen or dishonored without appalling reprisals and bloodshed. Many of the narrative poems in the tradition deal with incidents of this kind. Ylber, whose sister has been carried off by the prince (killing their eight brothers in the process), kicks the prince into insensibility before cutting off his head, then—because his sister has gone over to the enemy— drenches her hair in fish-oil and burns her to death. The folk-hero Gjeto-basho Muji, who has been offered by rich General Petr a whole merchant-ship stocked with precious things as bridewealth for his daughter Hajkuna, feels so dishonored by the offer that he slays the entire wedding party and sends Petr, humiliated, into exile (and keeps the ship).

There is a starkness and dry tragic irony in these poems that reminds us of the finest of Thomas Hardy's literary ballads or the mordant and laconic wit of such Icelandic saga heroes as Skarpheddin in *Burnt Njal*. These characters are absolutely certain of who they are, and their identity is unrelenting machismo. They stroke their mustaches before they speak but act with appalling suddenness. What distinguishes them from their counterparts in other ballad traditions is the element of ruthless sly cunning. Lord William in the Douglas Tragedy gets his death-wound killing all seven of Margaret Douglas' brothers together with her father in an attempted elopement, but his tragedy has a sad Celtic ring unlike the canny ferocity of the Illyrian hero Muji. As another poem puts it, in a classic mountain epithalamium:

> Bridey, bridey, sweet and coy,
> Mount the pony,
> Bear a boy,

Name him Paladin, for joy.

Like the paladin of Hotit,
To God's vow he'll be devoted;
Like the paladin of Grudë,
He'll be brave and wise and good;
Like the paladin of Kelmend,
Harvest legends without end;
Like the paladin of Kastrat,
You'll find nobody like that;
Like the paladin of Shkrel,
Trickier than sprites from Hell!

The paladin of Shkrel is the punchline. Perhaps the analogy is the Mafia wedding celebrated by Coppola in *The Godfather*. The hero, like Homer's Odysseus, is here conflated with the trickster.

It is not only the males who guard women's honor with violence. In "Kolë's Peerless Women" Dranë avenges an attempt on her honor by Gjin Ndresa with a quick shot from her faithful pistol while they are talking it over afterward. And she warns the judge, before whom she is brought for the murder, that there is another bullet meant for him if he does not acquit her.

Any society in which the opposite sex is a forbidden object guarded by dangerous protectors is going to be a pressure cooker for sexual passion. The Albanian folk poets evoke with appalling frankness the pain and existential vividness of desire, and recognize with a clear-eyed tragic honesty the ruthless politics of love. In these politics the women often seem to have the upper hand:

BEAUTY WITH A WHITE SHAWL

"Hey, beauty in your milkwhite shawl,
Have those breasts budded out at all?"
"They started just a week ago,
A week, I think, maybe a year.
They've got bad habits as they grow,
They're hard, and they stick out to here.
My bodice chafes them, and they flow
With sherbet if you touch them, so."

"Now won't you give some to the squire,
Some of that sweet stuff to me?"
"I'll save it for a boy with fire,
Young, unmarried, young and free,
Someone who will rise much higher,
Who sings and plays his flute for me."

This apparent freedom, however, exists in the context of a system is which a father can make his daughter marry a rich and nasty old man:

MARTA GOSSIPS

Marta tells the girls that please her:
"Poor wife saddled with a geezer.
Daddy wed me to this oldie,
Buried me alive with Moldy.
Nothing's worse than when you face
Death's-head by the fireplace.
Sixty years went to create
Gray-bush beard and barren pate.

16

Drool is all he gives, or worse:
Daddy, here's a daughter's curse."

But fierce and lasting love can emerge from the repression and
the explosive physical passion of these mountain people:

HEY, BEAUTIFUL!

"Beauty by the flowerbed,
Head up like a thoroughbred,
Hear what I have got to say:
If I catch you, caught you'll stay.
I have got a heavy jones,
I've a yen to jump your bones,
Pink cheeks, breasts as white as snow,
Two big handfuls, just like so,
Damned if I will let them go!"
"Suck my white tits, young Sir Randy?
You'd go crazy, like they're brandy,
Kill somebody, like enough,
Then go home to sleep it off."
"I'd kill twenty, literally,
Just to lie upon your belly —
Where'd you get those cheeks I see?"
"Almighty God gave them to me,
Given me by God Almighty:
Partly fat and partly meaty,
Partly muscle, partly fatty,
Just to please my latest sweetie,
Just to keep my lover happy —
But he must be young and peppy,
So that when I hear his call,

17

I will let my dinner fall,
I will leave my own grave-dust
To be the roadmap of his chest —
But I hope we will both die
On the same night, you and I;
And we'll lie there, grave by grave —
Who needs Heaven if you've love?"

Though the mountain people are nominally Christian —
and very pious, too, in their fierce way — they still maintain
underneath the Christian patina the ancient paganism of central
Europe. One of the hero Muji's adventures concerns the witches
of the mountains, who bear a strong resemblance to the Norns
and the Fates. A significant genre of their poetry is the spell or
incantation, which preserves very old forms of polytheism and
totemism. An example:

SONG OF THE SALT

Whoo, whoo, black bear,
Whoo, whoo, white bear.
Whoo, spellbinder,
Earthborn pixie,
Water-nixie,
May the weak mind
And the strong mind
Melt in songlines,
Where is healing,
There is fortune.
Whoo, whoo, whoo!

The bears in this one sound distinctly Neolithic. This is the

18

incantation for a divination ritual, in which the diviner sprinkles salt on his palm, then takes two hairs from his client's head, crosses them over the salt, and then places over them a coin taken at random by the client from his pocket (which will be the diviner's fee). The diviner then squeezes his hand, blows on the contents, and reads the shapes suggested by the salt. The "whoo" sound in the poem represents the blowing.

These are, in fact, the themes of the traditional pastoral — naïve love, the celebration of the land and the shepherd's life, the emblematic contrasts of old and young, city and country, the lament of the lover, the satire on human nature, the magical forces of nature, the cruelty of the fair maid. These shepherds, then, are not unlike their colleagues a few hundred miles south and seventeen centuries earlier, whose Arcadian lives were celebrated by the Hellenistic bucolic poets Theocritus, Bion, and Moschus.

Hearing and translating these Albanian folk poems is like encountering for the first time the astonishing limestone landscapes of the river Li in China: suddenly we realize that the strange little sugarloaf mountains in the ancient scrolls were not, after all, some conventional symbolism for the arcadian countryside but the literal, representative truth. Certainly the pastoral poets (on down through Virgil and Sannazaro, Marot and Ronsard, Sidney, Shakespeare, and Marvell) clean up the shepherd's act a little, as the Chinese poets clean up the pine forests and little pavilions on the crags — but they are not exaggerating the frank intensity of the native oral poetry they imitate. Lord and Parry were astonished to find Homeric epic in modern Serbia; the American collectors of country music found old-world Scots-Irish heroes in the guise of cowboys; here we can find ancient pastoral still surviving in the mountains of Illyria.

But pastoral is not the only genre represented in the Albanian folk tradition. There are, besides, poems that might best be called anthems in praise of regional or national identity and invocations of God's aid to it; heroic ballads about individual named adventurers and fighters; and what might be the makings of an epic, in the cycle of longer heroic poems telling of the exploits of Gjeto-basho Muji.

Given the rich materials outlined here, how can they be translated into English? One fundamental problem, that of course a written poem is not the same as a (partly improvised) oral poem, has already been mentioned. The ethical issue is in a sense moot, since human practice in general has been to render oral materials into literate form, and some of the greatest works of human genius, such as the *Iliad*, the *Mahabharata*, and the *Popol Vuh*, have been the result. And this problem contains the glimmerings of a solution to other problems, such as the faithful rendering of the tone, style, sound and ethos of the original.

The key is what English and Albanian have in common, that is, prosody, with all its rich indications of stress, rhythm, musical tone, meter, and rhyme. Gjekë Marinaj and I resolved to reproduce as exactly as possible the metrical form and rhyming patterns of the original, believing that if an English-speaking audience hears the sound of the original — both its basic beat and its characteristic variations — the emotional content will at least in part come through.

The rules of metrical form may in fact have originated in all the literate cultures as an attempt, at the point of the introduction of literacy, to analyze and reproduce exactly the sound and emotional emphasis of the original oral poetry. Today the most reliable guide to, for instance, Elizabethan pronunciation is the implicit map to it that is provided by the rhyme sounds and metrical emphasis of Tudor poetry. So in attempting to match the sound of the Albanian poems we are, as it were, reproducing the efforts of any nation's scholars to preserve its oral poetry into the era of literary communication and record. That is, the prosody and meter of literary poetry is its oral element, preserved almost like a tape recording or a musical score—literate poetry is a dry and robust container for the volatile and fugitive potion of its oral essence.

A few years ago Marinaj and I conceived the project. Originally we were to have gone together to Albania, but illness prevented me from making the trip. Marinaj, however, traveled alone deep into the mountains of Albania, relying on his own background as a child of mountain farming parents and his considerable reputation as a national poet to gain entry into the inns and coffee-houses where local and itinerant poets give their recitations. Marinaj is known in Albania as an authentic dissenter against the brutal Communist regime under which he grew up (and which only fell in 1991). His poem "Horses" slipped by the censors because of its metaphorical subtlety and was published in a major literary periodical. Albania, like a few other odd countries around the world, is mad for poetry, and the intelligent oppressed national audience soon realized what the censors had missed—the poem imaged the Albanian people as the patient brutalized horses of a cruel master. This then became clear to the regime. To save his life Marinaj had to escape into exile at night over the mountains, pursued by the state secret police, abandoning his promising career as a major cultural media figure. So my co-translator had credentials of his own, which were readily appreciated by his brother and sister poets in the mountain hamlets. All doors were open to him.

Using new portable computing and recording technology, Marinaj photographed the poets, the landscape, and the venues of oral performance. He took notes on the names, locations,

21

and backgrounds of the oral performers and made recordings of the long and often festive evenings of poetry. Snatches of conversation, music, and ad hoc commentary are also preserved in the process; and the whole collection, compiled under huge difficulties and at some personal sacrifice, is I believe an extraordinary and valuable achievement.

Our collaborative work begins with listening to the recording together, often with reference to photographs of the poet and the scene, and sometimes concluding with a final decision as to whether this particular work is of the quality that we want for our first selected volume (there is much more in Marinaj's archive than is needed). Hearing the recording, I am able at once to score and scan it and identify the meter and rhyme scheme, picking up a good deal—though I have only a few words of Albanian—about the tone, mood, style, and music of the poem. Marinaj used to provide a written trot for the poems, but we since found it unnecessary—Marinaj's software enables us to hear the poem line by line, upon which he gives orally an instant literal translation. I usually inquire about the nature of the language—is it archaic, rural, noble, urbane, colloquial, epigrammatic, biblical, humorous, learned, scatological, neologistic, polite, "poetic," vulgar, technical, etc? Is it in a local dialect, does it involve puns or suggestive assonances or multiple meanings? I write down a rough English version of what I hear, together with some variants and cognates if there is an ambiguity. Albanian grammar and word order are not unlike English, which makes it easier in that respect than, say, German, Hungarian, and Chinese, in my experience.

I then take the result home and render it into the same metrical form and rhyme-pattern in English as the original, taking care to include variations and metrical reversals in about the same ratio as in the Albanian, and attempting to find the

22

same diction register in the English as in the Albanian. I make no attempt to "Anglicise" the language or bring it up to date if, as many of these oral poems do, they contain archaisms indicative of earlier versions of it and concomitant traditional worldviews. For instance, the word "bardhë" as applied to a woman is, I believe, cognate with and properly translated by the archaic/poetic English word "fair." I do not try to modernize it to "beautiful" or literalize it to "pale" or "white" lest the social and even moral implications of the old word be lost.

I then share the draft of the finished version with Marinaj at our next meeting, and make needed corrections. Matters of judgment often come up, for instance where it becomes obvious to one of us that a later poet has at some point interpolated disparate material into a finely-honed old poem or has forgotten an essential plot point in a longer poem. For instance, in the strange and supernatural poem "Muji and the Three Witches," which exists in other known oral versions, the reciter of it has clearly forgotten and left out the key to breaking the spell of the golden goats, which is that they lose their magic if they drink human blood. Later in the recitation it becomes obvious to the reciter that he has erred, and he then, rather flustered, alters the ending to give the poem a different (and rather misogynistic) ending. In this case I, as another oral poet, so to speak, improvised a few lines to repair the damage and gave a construction of the ending that made more sense without altering the general literal meaning.

The canonical meter of Albanian folk poetry is the trochaic tetrameter rhyming couplet. It is varied by the addition of light syllables, including an extra one at the end to make a feminine ending, by using interlaced rhyme schemes instead of the couplet, and by the addition of several lines with the same rhyme to create a climax. As an example of the last, in "Poor

Hysen," a rich young man has just bought the beautiful wife of a bankrupt and married her, but he learns to his horror, after the marriage is consummated, that his second-hand bride is his own long lost sister. She (like Jocasta in *Oedipus*) tries to help him escape his fate, but the relentless rhymes, so to speak, draw them to the shocking conclusion:

> Now to comfort him, she tried
> Questioning him of his mother:
> "Poor man, did you have a sister?"
> "Wretched girl, had you a brother?"
> "I left behind a little brother
> With a birthmark like a blister
> On his forehead, from his mother."
> Lightning-fast, he fetched a light,
> Raised his cap to show the sight:
> There the mark was, red and white.
> So embracing, they begin
> To weep the fate that made them kin.

Another example might help clarify the power of poetic form as a key element of poetic meaning and a vital guide to translation. One of the favorite devices of the Albanian oral poet is the repetition of a line but in reverse grammatical order for emphasis, while preserving the metrical rhythm, as here:

> I'll not give up my guns alive,
> My guns I'll not give up alive!

In another poem, delightfully reminiscent of Chaucer's "The Nun's Priest's Tale," this technique is used for comic effect, partly to mimic the sound of the chickens who are speaking:

24

THE PROUD ROOSTER

Twelve red hens were dancing, dancing,
Dancing, dancing, twelve red hens;
Picked a bride for that proud rooster,
For that rooster picked a bride:
Chose for him an ancient chicken
Ancient chicken chose for him.
But that rooster lost his temper,
Lost his temper, that proud cock.
"I don't want that ancient chicken,
No old chicken do I want."
Cock-a-doodle, cock-a-deedle,
Cock-a-deedle, cock-a-doodle.

Twelve red hens were dancing, dancing,
Dancing, dancing, twelve red hens.
Picked a bride for that proud rooster,
For that rooster picked a bride.
Now they chose a sweet young pullet,
Sweet young pullet now they chose.
Then the proud cock was right merry,
Merry was that proud cock then.
"How I love that sweet young pullet,
How I love that sweet young pullet,
She is just the bride for me,
She is just the bride for me."
Cock-a-deedle, cock-a-doodle,
Cock-a deedle, cock-a-doodle.

At the end of the poem the resolution of the discord between
the rooster and his hens is indicated formally by the restoration

of concordant word order in the last six lines.

Though the trochaic tetrameter is as dominant in Albanian folk poetry as the iambic pentameter in traditional English literary poetry and the ballad form in English folk poetry, it makes room for many other forms; and the clear distinction among them and the difference of their rhythm can help guide the translator in individualizing the poems. Too often even sensitive and nuanced free verse translations of metered originals can have the effect of reducing everything to the same international aesthetic. The difference from the trochaic tetrameter can clearly be seen in the following examples:

MILKING-TIME

> Milk sweet, milk sweet!
> Pail full from the sheep's warm teat.
> Milk sweet, milk sweet
> From the valleys where they eat.
> Milk sweet, milk sweet
> Where they dream upon their feet.
> Milk sweet, milk sweet,
> Youth's and age's living heat:
>
> Milk sweet! Milk sweet!

This is an ancient chanting measure:

> / /, / /
> /-/-/-/

—and it carries a flavor of great chthonic antiquity. The following verses from "Shepherd's Song" are different again,

26

clearly a call-and-response song:

> Why, oh why, does the shepherd cry?
> Cry, Shepherd, cry:
> The wolf is in the fold, that's why;
> Cry, shepherd, cry.
> The teeming ewes, throat-bitten, die;
> Cry, shepherd, cry;
> The unborn lambs are lost for aye,
> Cry, shepherd, cry.
> It bit his fingers off today,
> Cry, shepherd, cry,
> So now his flute he'll never play,
> Cry, shepherd, cry.

The meter, with variations, is basically as follows:

> -/-/-/-/
> /, /-/

The trochaic tetrameter couplet is a folk meter well suited to swift narrative with an unrelenting onward energy:

> /-/-/-/(-) A
> /-/-/-/(-) A

Versions of it can be found in Lonnrot's *Kalevala*, which echoes and compiles Finnish folk epic, and Longfellow's *Hiawatha*, a neglected masterpiece that with great learning simulates a folk form. Contrast it with the English ballad form, in which the iambic tetrameter alternates with the iambic trimeter:

-/-/-/-/ A
-/-/-/ B
-/-/-/-/ A or C
-/-/-/ B

— as in the Ballad of Chevy Chase:

> God prosper long our noble king,
> Our lives and safeties all!
> A woeful hunting once there did
> In Chevy Chase befall.
>
> To drive the deer with hound and horn
> Earl Percy took his way;
> The child may rue that is unborn
> The hunting of that day!

A naïve translator might want to use the English ballad meter to translate Albanian heroic folk poetry, on the theory that it evokes the same socio-cultural space. But such a decision would, I believe, be a mistake, because it would ignore the difference in basic texture and music between the two metrical forms, a difference that is prosodic, transcends the bounds of the strictly linguistic, and is based on natural human universals. The English ballad comes to a conclusion and resolution at the end of each four-line stanza, a conclusion with a dying fall as the shorter three-stress line comes to the final rhyme. The Albanian trochaic tetrameter drives onward with a restless energy, as here in "Zek Jakini":

> Ali summons his vizier;
> With the horn he always carries,

28

Calls up all his janissaries,
Beckons Kul Bektelin there.
Soon enough Bektelin came,
With his golden sword of fame.
And Bektelin came to Trush,
This the city he would crush.
But Jakini fears him not —
Son of a fiery patriot:
Grabs his rifle by the breech:
"God give just deserts to each!"
And now parley Kul and Zek:
"Death is rushing on us here —
Let us fight like Tuç and Lek,
Let us be sung like brave Gjinlek"...

As a result, Albanian narrative poems often end with a suddenness that is shocking even when the story as such is complete. There is rarely an epigrammatic or sententious summing-up as there often is in Anglo-Saxon folk poetry. The epigrammatic force is certainly there in Albanian poetry, but it is usually given to something said by one of the characters.[1]

In traditional English verse, as I have already noted, there was from early days a distinction between the "high" urban cosmopolitan educated voice of the iambic pentameter and the

---

[1] Some of the longer Albanian oral narrative poems abandon the strict trochaic form and use a sort of rhythmic free verse, not especially trochaic, with four major stresses, which I have represented by a loose blank verse, an iambic pentameter that lightens or suppresses one of the heavier syllables. But it is still memorable enough for the oral poets to recite/improvise in the way that Lord and Parry observed in Serbian epic verse, using stock phrases and epithets and sticking to a story with a number of possible digressions depending on the amount of time available. I believe that some of the tragic and heroic "bite" of these poems is lost by being so translated, and have sometimes felt that I would prefer to render them into the classic tetrameter, even if by doing so I would falsify the metrical form of the original. But the stories these poems tell are usually so striking, graphic, horrific, and moving in themselves that perhaps the heavy beat of the tetrameter over a long period would be unbearable in addition.

29

"low" rural provincial unlatined (and even illiterate) voice of the 4-3-4-3 ballad form. This class distinction can be seen in other literatures, too, the alexandrine and the endecasillabo playing in French and Italian the same role as the English iambic pentameter. Medieval popular Latin verse, based on stress, and often in trochaic tetrameter ("Dies irae, dies illa"), existed in a social space below the quantitative classical poetry of the ancient Romans and Greeks. But Albanian poetry seems to share with the Chinese classical poetry the peculiar feature that for most of its history it never diverged into high and low styles. Albanian and Tang poetry is both "high" and "low," and there is no difference in metrical form between the voices. I believe the reasons for this similarity are quite different, however. Albanian society was in a class sense beheaded by the Turks — its upper courtly and cosmopolitan class was replaced by Turkish beys and administrators. Thus poetry had no chance to formally separate in terms of class. Chinese Tang society, however, was so dominated by the mandarin class at all levels, a class of people chosen by examination for their poetic gifts from the whole population, that a separate folk tradition never got a chance to emerge into the light before it was coopted into the clerical class.[2]

Beyond all technical and sociological considerations,

---

[2] The fact that the examination for the mandarinate was in theory open to all if they could find the time and resolve to learn the Chinese characters may also have fostered a certain egalitarian noblesse oblige among the literate. The great poet Bai Juyi, it is said, tested his poetry on the illiterate cleaning woman—if she did not understand it, he would rewrite it. Interestingly, the two dominant verse forms in Tang poetry are the seven-syllable line (corresponding in rhythm to the English ballad form) and the five-syllable line (corresponding to the iambic pentameter). If there had been a tendency in Chinese poetry to diverge formally based on class, this difference would have provided an obvious marker. But there is no discernible difference in class or elevation between the diction and subject matters of the two forms. And in Albanian poetry the tetrameter couplet serves for the most vulgar and jocular purposes as for the most solemn, heroic, and tragic.

however, is the living presence of a vital folk tradition that is still reproducing itself in the hills of Albania. The work of Gjekë Marinaj and myself has been to find in English the ancient energies to introduce that presence and aura, those "dark sounds" of Balkan *duende*, into the academic and perhaps over-sophisticated realms of modern poetry in English.

THE POEMS

PATRIOTIC SONGS

HOMAGE TO THE WARRIORS

When I take my lute to sing
Snow-peaks perch upon my string,
And the forest heights fall still
And the starry heavens chill
And the ice-fields and the crests
Come to sing the heroes' gests.
Words like water from the spring
Teach the heroes' deeds to sing;
Green-clad hillsides raise the call
Echoed from the mountain-wall.

Time harrows rocks and stones and all,
Yet heroes for the flag still fall;
The Cemi brook runs red with gore,
But their mothers will bear more.
They give birth to bravery,
Let the Alban eagles fly.

THE EAGLE OF ALBANIA

Mighty bird and mighty burden,
May your quills and pennons shine,
That you shall not be forgotten,
In our flag we set your sign.
In our hearts we set your scars,
Set your laughter, set your wars;
In a sunbeam's golden glory
We recall your glowing story...!

THE PLEDGE OF THE HILL-FOLK

This our vow we shall not fail,
Our high hills are not for sale:
We would die to guard the pale.

Man's vow is God's vow unseen.
Little do the Turk's guns mean:
We're the powder-magazine.

God's vow is man's vow exalted,
Earth by pure hearts' salt is salted:
Flag-vow over earth is vaulted.

Oath to oath and hand to hand,
Mountain-snow on mountain-land:
Wherefore fights this Malsor-band?

Lightning-like, the Turks they scorn,
Die as if they're being born,
By their faith and nation drawn.

THE CURSE

He who greets the occupier,
Blast his house with lightning-fire.
Weaver of his velvet bands,
May God cut off both his hands.
Knitter of the tyrant's hose,
Wither her arms that made his clothes.
Shkoder-man who helps those ones:
May his house beget no sons.

IN THE MOUNTAINS OF TARAMIS

In the heights of Taramis
Speaks the Aura of Malësisë.
I drink the mountains with my eyes,
I sing the hills where homeland lies,
I sing the skies the Aura flies:

"In the mountains where it snows
No doctor needs to show his nose,
Apothecaries we don't need,
No medicines at all, indeed:
Where at noon the sun won't burn,
Where winds dance with the waving fern,
Where the grasses sweetly sing,
Strawberries ripen in the spring,
Where the shepherd's song is merry,
Drinking milk with sweet strawberry
Iced with snow and berry-fresh,
That renews an old man's flesh,
Turns an old man to a young,
Makes his feet so swift and strong,
He climbs mountains all day long.

"Of other places I might speak,
With bogs and ditches dank and bleak,
Where barren wastelands breed disease,
Malarias and maladies,
And medicine's the people's ease.
All my words are good and true:
Where sick sheep drool and sick goats spew,
People never can get well;

Where the sky is dark as hell,
And mosquitoes, ticks and fleas
And horseflies rule the leafless trees,
And many-footed insects suck,
And leeches grip you in the muck,
And children shriek "Kuku nanë!"
Outdoors and indoors every day:
Better for them that they had not
Such parents as would let them rot.

"Of city people I might tell,
But they self-advertise too well.
They eat less, it is very true,
But they have so much less to do.
They are so scared that they will die,
They live where doctors are nearby.
No young man here is such a chump,
He knows a good place from a dump,
Summers he hikes up in the hills,
Comes down in winter from the chills,
That's why our youth is strong and hale,
Not short and skinny, thin and frail;
They do not lack mustache or beard,
And their looks are justly feared,
They make you feel a feeble beast—
They don't need money in the least!"

I won't go on—I've said my piece;
If you don't live here in Malësi,
Nothing's easy, even dying,
You should give up even trying:
Hear the Aura's final plea:

42

"You might as well go peacefully,
And hand in hand, as blind fools see,
Go drown yourselves down in the sea."

MY HOME VILLAGE

Homeland, do not hang your head,
Though I left that night, and fled:
I bequeathed to you my house,
One day I'll return, to rest
Forever in your gentle breast.

Lovely Qeparo, your rill
Runs down between hill and hill,
Crowned with your last mountain height,
Bosom clothed with snow so white
You are Circe in the night.

You are to life, as life to love.
The brook's lips kiss the rocks above.
Your body, comet-shaped, streams light,
The whole world envies you, and I
Must return to you to die.

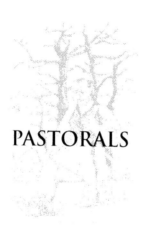

PASTORALS

MILKING-TIME

Milk sweet, milk sweet!
Pail full from the sheep's warm teat.
Milk sweet, milk sweet
From the valleys where they eat.
Milk sweet, milk sweet
Where they dream upon their feet.
Milk sweet, milk sweet,
Youth's and age's living heat:

Milk sweet! Milk sweet!

CHEESE

Bright curd, white curd,
With the finest rennet stirred,
Round, white, well-stored,
All the town will get the word!

BUTTER

Churn, churn, churnabumble,
Pour the milk and hear it tumble,
Churn, churn, churnabumble,
Sweetly let the plunger rumble.
Churn, churn, churnabumble,
Winking eyeballs from the mold,
Churn, churn, churnabumble,
Secret to the shepherd told,
Churn, churn, churnabumble:
Butter is the shepherd's gold.

SHEPHERD'S SONG

Why, oh why, does the shepherd cry?
Cry, Shepherd, cry:
The wolf is in the fold, that's why;
Cry, shepherd, cry.
The teeming ewes, throat-bitten, die;
Cry, shepherd, cry;
The unborn lambs are lost for aye,
Cry, shepherd, cry.
It bit his fingers off today,
Cry, shepherd, cry,
So now his flute he'll never play,
Cry, shepherd, cry.

The shepherd sings on hill and dale,
Joy to us, oh joy;
He's got fresh ewes to fill his pail:
Joy to us, oh joy.
Udder-milk he'll mix with soil,
 —Joy to us, oh joy—
Glue his fingers whole and hale,
Joy to us, oh joy.
Now he'll play his flute so well,
Joy to us, oh joy,
Sheep will bleat, woods tell the tale,
Joy to us, oh joy!

THE PROUD ROOSTER

Twelve red hens were dancing, dancing,
Dancing, dancing, twelve red hens;
Picked a bride for that proud rooster,
For that rooster picked a bride:
Chose for him an ancient chicken
Ancient chicken chose for him.
But that rooster lost his temper,
Lost his temper, that proud cock.
"I don't want that ancient chicken,
No old chicken do I want."
Cock-a-doodle, cock-a-deedle,
Cock-a-deedle, cock-a-doodle.

Twelve red hens were dancing, dancing,
Dancing, dancing, twelve red hens.
Picked a bride for that proud rooster,
For that rooster picked a bride.
Now they chose a sweet young pullet,
Sweet young pullet now they chose.
Then the proud cock was right merry,
Merry was that proud cock then.
"How I love that sweet young pullet,
How I love that sweet young pullet,
She is just the bride for me,
She is just the bride for me."
Cock-a-deedle, cock-a-doodle,
Cock-a deedle, cock-a-doodle.

51

HEROIC TALES

DEDË LUL TOMA

Dedë Lul Toma, without peer,
Splendid in his boots and gear,
Flies across the rock-ribbed fells
To the hall where the king dwells.
He seizes a guitar and so
Plays a song of grief and woe.
How his eyes roll to and fro!—
Grinding millstones scarce turn so.
"King, it's you I've come to see.
Just a few words, two or three,
I have now that must be said:
I have heard that you have wed."
"The seven seas my witness be,
Your daughter truly married me."
"In our code is not implied
Two men marry but one bride.
Without wedding feast and banns,
No woman can become a man's.
In our tradition no girl may
Choose to give herself away."
He put his hand upon his "Ten,"
Ten times he stopped his firing then,
Left the king lifeless on the floor,
Left him dead forevermore.
On the king's table blood still flows;
"You are surrounded," Toma knows,
Around the room his sharp eye ranges,
He tears a door from off its hinges,
Strikes one man down and kicks another;
Till shattered men are heaped together,

And flees across the mountain's limb—
No bullet can catch up with him.
At last he halts, somewhere, nowhere;
His conscience sits in judgment there:
"How could I do this dreadful thing?
What shame shall these dark doings bring?
How could I kill our only king?
In such a slaughter what is good,
To drench the king's hall with his blood?
And if I venture home, I fear
My mother's dreadful curses there:
She'll give no place to make a stand,
King's men will come swiftly, and
Take my wife and children; then
All my lands will go to ruin.
My brother Gjergj they'll cruelly hale
Through streets behind a horse's tail,
Running a gauntlet I deserved."
Now Dedë all his courage nerved,
And so surrendered to the Bey,
Who was a good man, by the way.
He offered neither blows nor shame;
At his command a droshky came
To carry Dedë straightway to Vlorë
Where wise physicians might explore
How to heal Dedë forevermore.
Some thought him dead, condoled with Gjergj:
"Your pity, friends, pray do not urge;
Until I see him in the grave,
I know the Bey his crime forgave
And won't betray my brother brave:
He feigned Dedë's death, his life to save."

KOLË'S PEERLESS WOMEN

Mountain-man, young Gjin Ndreca,
Long had been a troublemaker.
Now he raided Kolë Marku,
Broke the gate of Kolë Marku,
Broke into his sheepfold seeking
Anything thought worth his taking:
Copper sheep-bells from the rams,
Tender lambs beneath their dams,
Oxen from the manger's side,
Kolë's son's newly-wedded bride.

So on market-day there came
Kolë's fair women, high in fame;
Gjin Ndreca they confronted,
Him who had their virtue hunted:
"Mountain thing, you flee in vain
Those whose honor you would stain."
Said Dranë Noja — dear God, hear her! —
"My duty's in this derringer."
Like a millstone see her spin,
Draw a gun and shoot that Gjin.
Gjin Ndreca little kenned
Woman's hand would be his end;
Gjin Ndreca knew the rocks,
Knew the mountains like a fox,
Knew a fighting-man's quick fire:
Did not know a woman's ire.

Comes a wagon with an order:
Dranë must come to court in Shkoder,

"Long life to you, your Honor, surely,
Make your judgments well and truly.
Ask in Breg të Matës, Gorre;
Ask about Ndreca's story.
Ask them what he did to us,
Ask and then consider thus:
Oft he stole an ox or cow,
Never honor, until now.
Mine was the first he stole," she said,
"So I live and he is dead.
What use bullets, but to kill
Him who would your honor steal.
Judge against us and you will
Get one for yourself as well."

YLBER

When that wife was made a widow,
God had left her ten poor orphans,
Nine boys and a girl, they say.
Hard it was alone to raise them,
Begging door to door she fed them,
Clothed with thorn-snagged wool their bodies:
God sent hardships every day.
She begs, but nothing do they give her,
Fatherless, they're bound to die.

Mourning Dove asks her poor orphans,
"Listen, fatherless, say I:
To the market we'll take Ylber,
Offer Ylber to a buyer,
That nine live, let one be lost,
For if not we starve and die:
I beg, but never find a giver."
Burning, grieving, they agree
To take and sell the youngest boy:
So that whole night passed away.

Early the mother rose next day,
Dressed him pleasing to the eye,
To the bazaar took him away,
And in the merchant's hands she dropped the boy.

But seeing him, he would not buy.
Along now came the new lord Bey,
Selim Spahiu was his name.
Selim came close up to the boy

And loved the beauty of his face.
"Wretched mother, what's his price?"
"Three hundred ducats," said the dame.
From his pouch he counted then
Three hundred ducats in a trice:
Selim took the poor lad home.

Seizing the gold, in tears she came
Where the other children waited.
With what care she raised those children! —
Bought them land and lawns and garden,
Built them dwellings, house and mansion;
Eight fine brothers grew to manhood,
Swiftly God had made them wealthy.
But the girl became a beauty,
Snow-White the Fair was her nickname;
Distant soon had spread her fame:
To the Magyar prince it came.
A mighty army now he gathered,
Broke into the widow's homestead,
Slew all eight sons she had mothered,
Seized Snow-White and, when he'd gone,
Left the widow all alone.

Poor woman, she can't stop her shrieking,
Night and day she weeps unceasing
Till both eyes are stricken blind.
Nightmare was it just to hear her,
Lips agape and unconfined.

Thirty drovers happened by;
Hearing her, up spoke their chief:

"In the name of God, dear comrades,
I'll go in that house, or try,
For the screaming never ceases."
In the house amid the ashes
There he found her in her grief.
"In God's name who gave you life,
What great trouble can afflict you
That your crying never ceases,
That your eyes are stricken blind?"

Hear now how she turns to answer!
"Cease I cannot, such need drives me:
Ten poor orphans God had left me,
Begging door to door I raised them,
Such a hard life God had sent me,
With my orphans bound to die.
My youngest I must take to market,
Sold him for three hundred ducats;
So the nine were saved thereby.
I bought land and field and garden,
Built them dwellings, house and mansion,
Eight fine sons and one fair daughter.

"But God sent the Magyar Prince
And he fell upon the homestead,
Put my eight sons to the slaughter,
Sacrilegious, seized my daughter,
And with him went then my daughter,
I—Mourning Dove—left all alone.
Young man, in God's name, might you be
A traveler?"
And he replied:

"Yes, a drover's life I lead."
Now she roused and spoke again:
"For God's sake who gave you being,
Since you go from town to town,
Tell my griefs to everyone —
Best, if you see him, to my son."

Now he got up to be going,
Told his comrades everything,
Told the tale from town to town,
Till he came to a tall inn,
Got a drink and then began
Telling the tale to everyone.
A young man leapt then to his feet
Came up to the storyteller,
Begged him that he might repeat
All that had been said and done —
Had the Prince cut down his brothers,
Had he snatched his sister's honor,
Left his mother all alone?

Aye, says the drover. — What of Selim?
Said Ylber to his foster-father:
"I can't beg you to release me,
I cost you a mighty ransom:
From my home you can forbid me
But my life would then oppress me
If I can't avenge my brothers,
Pay him back for my lost sister,
If I cannot see my mother."

Hear how Selim made his answer:

"Love bids me live with you forever
But I have no heart to keep you
From your mother's homestead, hold you
From avenging sister or brother."

Then the lad donned fine apparel,
Selim saddles him a courser,
Places in his hand a sword,
Holds back tears and says farewell;
Hand to hand those brave men part.
Selim offers one more word:
"All I gave you I absolve you:
This I swear before the Lord."

To his homestead then rode Ylber,
Found his mother still in mourning:
They embraced — such grief and yearning —
And he took her to the wise man,
And his mother's eyes got better.

Two maids hired he for his mother;
Then set out to seek the Prince,
Enters the Prince's battlements,
Finds his sister, knows her face,
Takes her, they say, in his embrace.

Gathering herself, she spoke:
"Brother, came you to take me away
And our brothers' blood repay?"
Ylber had but this to say:
"With such thoughts I have come hither."
Now the answer of his sister:

63

"For that I have an easy mind."

Then she gave him food and drink,
But she drugged her brother's wine,
And as instant as a wink
Sleep took him a prisoner.

To the window runs the sister,
And the prince, arriving, sees,
Runs to him, falls to her knees,
Trembling, gathers words and speaks:
"All for you I've caught my brother,
Do with him what is your pleasure;
For he would cut us asunder."

Then he finds the sleeping Ylber,
Manacles his hands and feet there,
Kicks him in the ribs, and taunts him:
"Don't you know your blackest day?"
As cut by sword, sleep fell away;
Ylber felt the tight chain pain him,
Knew his sister had betrayed him.

Snow-White no more, the sister said:
"You must cut off Ylber's head:
He would cut me off from you."
The Prince looked in her eye and said:
"Ylber's too young for me to slay—
I will not cut off his head.
I'll throw him in the stalls instead:
Mustangs will tear him till he's dead."
Hark how Ylber's mind now tricked them:

Sideways he lay in the mustangs' manger
And they neither bit nor kicked him:
Perhaps the Prince had thought he would.

But this sister rose up early,
Went to see how he had fared.
Here's what she flung at her lover:
"Ylber lives yet in your stable:
Had you heeded what I said,
'Tween his feet would be his head."
Looking askance at her he answered:
"This night will be cold and bitter.
To the cherry tree I'll rope him
Like a dog, in rain and snow:
Soon the boy's soul will escape him,
And your will accomplished so."

To the cherry tree he ties him,
Cold indeed the night God sent him,
Never ceased the bitter speaking
Of the rain and sleet and snow.

But God willed he should be rescued:
For the sister of the Prince
Rose up early on that morning,
Through the open window looking,
Faced the cold wind's violence;
But instead of cold felt warming,
Leaped out of the open window,
Wondered why earth did not wince.

Then and there she questions Ylber,

What he'd pay to save his life.
Ylber's closed his eyes, and spoken:
"I still have my strength and life."
Seizing him, the princess answers:
"If you give God's word forever
That you will make me your wife,
From that word will spring a lover
And together spring your life.
For us both I wish to save you,
And to pay for your eight brothers —
Life should not be caught and broken."

Ylber swears before the Lord:
"If in truth you save my life,
Were you blind, you'll be my wife."

Now the princess in her cunning
Drags a stump to the cherry-tree,
Throws a sheet on it, in seeming
Some poor prisoner to be.
Then she grasps his hand and leads him
To her chamber secretly;
Goes then to the Prince her brother
And with a cold look takes his eye.
 "That boy you tied to the cherry-tree
Is dead — I hope it gives you joy.
Now let me too have my pleasure:
Let me take his corpse to bury
In the Turkish cemetery."
Sweet and sour he gives her leave.

Cunning still, his sister planned it:

Set the tree-stump in a wagon,
Interred it in a Turkish grave
So no man would ever find it;
Thus the day began and ended.

Gaining in the human battle
With the powers of night and darkness,
Wise, the princess had arranged it,
Sets a sword in Ylber's hand.
Life in him burns more and more:
"That prince who debased my sister,
Must be stricken from the land."
Flies he to the Prince's door.

First the Prince's kicks he rendered,
Then he bade the man to stand;
With the sword his neck he sundered,
And the head rolled on the ground.
Like a stranded fish, now Ylber
Felt a darkness choking him:
And with fish-oil drenched his sister,
Laid to her hair a burning brand
So that she was burned to ashes.

Then he weds the Prince's sister,
Burns his palace, breaks his walls;
Safely they go to his mother,
Tell her "Your eight sons are paid;
Now in peace we'll live together."

WORD SPREADS IN ISTANBUL

Noc Mark Deda with this call
Curdles the peace of Istanbul:
"I'll not give up my guns alive,
My guns I'll not give up alive!
I'll wash the dales in blood that day
They come to take my guns away."
Young man with a double chin
Noc Mark's house would enter in;
His land is bony, the night is dark,
They beat the door of good Noc Mark.
Three deputies and one gendarme
Bellow at the sleeping farm:
"Noc Mark Deda, step outside,
Let's see your actions match your pride!
Orders our commandant gave:
Bring you in dead or alive."
"Give me five minutes more to sleep:
Tonight a holy night I keep."
Holy nights can swiftly pass:
Noc escapes, hides in his grass.
"God and St. Nicholas, may I
Survive their rage and see them die:
For my father I don't fear,
He is in his ninetieth year
And his time has come to die.
I'll avenge him — if not I,
Then my son or his son's son,
Till we've cut ten heads for one."

ZEK JAKINI

Gunshots echoed over the sea:
Murders in Trush, the word had run.
Zek Jakini took his gun,
Hastened to the butchery.
No blood-brother lacked his aid:
That was not how Zek was made.
He met three Malësor-men, consulted:
Challenged Ali Pasha then:
That the Bey be more insulted,
Sent a woman, not a man.
Ali summons his vizier;
With the horn he always carries,
Calls up all his janissaries,
Beckons Kul Bektelin there.
Soon enough Bektelin came,
With his golden sword of fame.
And Bektelin came to Trush,
This the city he would crush.
But Jakini fears him not—
Son of a fiery patriot:
Grabs his rifle by the breech:
"God give just deserts to each!"
And now parley Kol and Zek:
"Death is rushing on us here—
Let us fight like Tuç and Lek,
Let us be sung like brave Gjinlek."
Zek tells Kol Gjorit, his friend:
"Tight aim on Harop Sokolin,
Keep the muzzle on a bowline."
(Poor Martini-gun, to send

Many a brave man to his end.)
Kol replies to Zek Jakini:
"On his forehead hold your aim,
Hold it steady, shoot the same."
(Poor Martini, poor Martini,
Killing is a weary game.)
Kek's old mother screams "O woe!
Is he dead, and must I go
With no-one for to bake the dough?"
Fear not, mother, have no grief!
Zek slew all his foes, in brief:
Young Sokolin, the sharif,
And Bektelin, their great chief.

SUNG ACROSS THE SHOULDER

Hark to what the grapevine cries:
Tells Gjokova to arise,
Calls across the west wind's bluster:
Peja and Rugovë to muster!
Here's a hint from one who knows:
Troopship landing many foes,
Pouring out as black as crows.
Devil-may-care Zef Toma, see,
Was to hang on the mulberry tree —
For, they say, he did good work,
Avenged his uncles on the Turk--
As if to obey their order,
Rode his flying horse to Shkoder,
Where he saw them tie the noose;
So they scarcely could refuse
To grant his last wish — he made known:
"May the General alone
On the scaffold by the tree
Be the man who shall hang me."
This proud Pasha must agree.
Now the noose, between two faces,
Like a zero, quick, Zef places
On the Pasha's neck, and snap!
Kicks the lever of the trap.
What fine doctor, on that deck,
Can repair the Pasha's neck?
Zef leaps on his flying horse,
Homeward rides, and so of course —
Rugovë and Peja! Go to work
To save him from the crow-black Turk!

71

THE EPIC MATTER OF MUJI

THE MARRIAGE OF HAJKUNA

When Petr was promoted to a general
He wrote a letter fine and to the point
And sent it off to Muji in Judbinë.
"You are the famous Gjeto-Basho Muji.
I am so minded to marry me a wife.
If you will give me Hajkuna for my bride,
A merchant ship with moorage I will give you,
And in it there are seven market-stalls;
Its hold is full of finest merchandise,
Which you may sell wherever you may wish.
And you shall have a holy casket too
And in it is a chalice all of gold
And a clock circled with a golden serpent
With an enormous diamond in its mouth.
That diamond can illuminate a room
So that you do not need to light the lamps,
The diamond truly being lamp enough.
And in addition you shall be my kin —
If you but give Hajkuna to be mine."
Now Muji gets the letter and he reads it
And as he does so Muji grinds his teeth
And his hand finds its way toward his sword.
Halil watches his brother's agitation
And so when Muji puts the letter down
Halil strokes his mustache and speaks aloud:
"In the name of God who created you,
Brother, tell me whence that letter came
That made you grind your teeth like a rockslide
And caused your hand to wander to the sword."
Muji stroked his mustache and thus replied:

"Now God had better kill that General Petr
For what his mind has prompted him to do.
A letter fine and to the point he sent me—
Listen what he wrote in it to me.
If I give him Hajkuna for his wife
He will give me a merchant ship with moorage
That has in it seven market-stalls
And a hold full of finest merchandise,
And I may sell wherever I may wish;
He will give us that miraculous ark
That has in it the wondrous clock of gold,
And round the clock a golden snake has coiled
With an enormous diamond in its mouth
So bright that it will light up all the night
So that there is no need to light the lamps."
Halil strokes his mustache and thus replies:
"If you will listen, hear what I advise:
A simple switch could do the trick for us.
He wants our honor; we, though, will take his.
Let us accept whatever he now offers—
Except Hajkuna never will be his.
Let us make these conditions for the wedding:
He must bring all he offered in advance;
When he arrives ashore, among the bridesmaids
Must be his sister, the Countess Gjelinë.
We give them honor and fair entertainment,
Then when it's time the wedding party leaves
We place our General Petr at the head;
Between each man of his, set one of ours;
Then we will let them know what's on our mind.
O yes indeed there will be one fine marriage;
But I'm the one who'll marry fair Gjelinë

While our Hajkuna kicks the man and leaves him."
So Muji now did as he was advised.
With this in mind, he wrote out his reply;
The letter flies to General Petr's hand:
"When the day comes for you to claim your bride,
We will receive three hundred of your guests.
Let fair Countess Gjelinë be one of them.
Come and enjoy our city of Judbinë."
Muji set out to give his daughter honor
And called the bridal helper to prepare her.
Halil, her younger brother, comes on in
To the fresh-painted white room where she sits
Gives her the wedding-raiment thick with gold
That General Petr had brought by for her.
When she puts on the garments, how she screams! —
"From whence has come such fancy clothes as these?"
Halil strokes his mustache and says to her:
"Hajkuna, there is nothing you need fear;
Much riches we have won, and more will win,
With the Countess Gjelinë, whom I will marry."
And then Hajkuna understood it all.
When it was time the wedding guests would leave,
Muji prepared three hundred of his men.
After the farewell handshakes, each fell in
Behind his counterpart, ready for battle.
General Petr was the first in line;
Behind him Talo Budalina stood.
The Count of Senjit was the second there,
Behind him there was Desde Osman Aga,
The third in line was Limo Bajraktari,
And there behind him, Zuko Bajraktari —
Three hundred picked men matched against three hundred.

They kept them company a little way.
Now Talo Budalina spoke these words:
"Hear me, and hear me well, dear General Petr:
Your waistcoat is so beautifully made,
Three hundred of our men have followed it
Who mean to play at war with you today."
Ah, Petr stroked his mustache then and said:
"That is a problem easily resolved"
And dips into his pouch and scoops out ducats
And tossing them upon the dusty ground
Tells Talo he can pick them up himself.
Poor Talo! He was not a wealthy man.
He lusted for those ducats on the ground
And so he bent to pick the money up.
And now behold how quickly Petr ran!
But Talo, swifter still, caught up with him.
Hear now what General Petr said:
"If you will spare my life then yours is made."
Talo strokes his mustache and answers him:
"By now your wedding party is all dead,
And your Countess Gjelinë, most like, with child,
And our Hajkuna flaunts your wedding garments,
And Muji and Halil possess your merchant ship.
Since you are proven so unworthy, I
Am going to let you go and keep your life,
But you must vow that you will change your name,
Or you had better start to dig your grave.
And you must go away at once in exile,
And be a commoner with common folk
In a strange place far from your kith and kin."
Now Petr's blood, at this, has turned to water,
But he has no chance but to take the offer.

78

Thus Petr learned the honor of Albania,
That it cannot be bought, its customs trampled;
Leave us alone, and we will like you well.

MUJI AND THE THREE WITCHES

The daughter of the King had been betrothed
In marriage to our Gjeto-basho Muji.
He's picked out thirty men to greet the King
And bring the bride in triumph to her wedding.
Sokol Halili was their chosen leader.
But Muji held them back and said these words.
"In God's name who created you, mark well:
Do not dismount while you pass through the mountains,
Do not allow your horses loose to play;
No one should dance, though it be customary;
You are forbidden to fire off your guns.
For mountain-witches live about the passes,
Whose magic can turn man and horse to stone."
And so the wedding-guests mount to their saddles
And set off on their journey to the King.

They passed safe through the mountains of the witches,
Remembering that they were not to dance
Nor loose the horses on the grass to play,
And draw back on their bridles as he told them;
And not one shot they fired at rock or tree,
And safe and sound they came then to the King.

They fetched the bride and set out for Judbinë,
And when they reached the mountains of the witches
No man dismounted there to celebrate.
This was not lost on Desde Ali Aga:
"I can't believe I see what I am seeing:
You aren't singing, don't get down to shoot.
As wedding guests we often cross this pass;

We always loosed our horses to go play,
We always took the time for target-shooting,
But nothing ill did ever yet befall."
Now when the wedding party heard his words
They let their horses loose to roll and play,
Started to dance more merrily than ever,
And soon their singing rose until it echoed,
Nor was the target-practice left undone.
It was not long, O no not long at all
Before there was a whistling in the trees,
Rising to shrieks in which the witches came,
And turned the wedding-party all to stone
And all their horses too. The three weird sisters
Pursued the bride, seized her and flew away.

Three days have passed, and three nights turned to dawn,
And in Judbinë no wedding-guests have come;
Something is burning now in Muji's blood.
"So what in darkness' name befell my guests?"
He dressed himself and girded on his belt
And mounted his white horse, and rode away,
Turning his mount toward the witches' mountains.

High, high in the mountains he has traveled,
Too deep, too deep, into the witches' realm;
He finds a hooked branch there and ties his horse
And carefully he now surveys the forest,
Hoping to catch the movements of the witches.
At length he spies a narrow little path,
And Muji took that passage through the trees
That led him to a spring with a wood flume
Where Muji stopped and hid himself away.

Some time now passed, not so much time at all,
And to that spring came down a fair young maiden.
Muji steps forth and thus addresses her:
"In God's name who created you, tell me,
What power brought you here into these mountains?
For whom do you come here to fetch this water?"
How sore, how sore indeed the girl now sighs:
"A curse'd God must have created me.
He had pledged me to Çetobasho Muji,
And thirty groomsmen he had sent for me,
And in these valleys we had stopped to rest;
The groomsmen then began to dance and play,
Started to sing their songs of celebration,
Fired off their guns at targets here and there.
It wasn't long, indeed not long at all,
Before the crags and forest started shrieking,
And out of that three mountain witches came.
They turned the happy groomsmen all to stone,
They turned the very horses too to stone,
And then they seized me and they brought me here.
Now I must live with them and care for them,
And carry water, work as their fire-tongs."

Now Muji stroked his mustache and responded.
"If you saw Muji, would you recognize him?"
She puts her hand upon her breast and bows:
"How could poor I pick out the great lord Muji,
When I have never seen him with my eyes?
But judging by my mother's words about him,
I wager he who speaks to me is he."
That very moment Muji laughed aloud.
"Indeed, my lady, I'm your very Muji.

If I enjoy the good luck that has marked me,
I'll find some way to bring you to Judbinë;
But you will have to listen to me closely.
When evening comes and you have set their table,
Make sure all three of them are sitting down,
Then ask them where the magic spell is hidden.
If you can then escape them with your life —
For they will either kill you or they'll tell you —
If worst comes, I'll be hidden in the attic —
Tomorrow at the same time meet me here."
She took her pails of water and returned.

The youngest witch looks in her eyes and asks:
"What took you so much time, my little beauty?"
With hand on breast the brave girl now replies:
"With all this rain that's fallen in the mountains,
The water's muddy, and I had to strain it."
Soon now the evening started to get dark.
The bride has cleaned and set the witches' table;
With hand on breast she now begins to speak.
"By this fair table, sacred to three great ladies,
I beg you, tell me where your spell is hidden."
At this the eldest witch fell in a frenzy,
The middle witch gave her a cruel kick,
The youngest spat on her — but all three said:
"Your beauty, little one, has saved your life."

Now they explain the secrets of the spell:
"Three golden goats live in the highest mountain.
They share the grass of Turks and infidels.
Their every lock of hair is purest gold,
Their horns are solid bullion through and through;

83

No one can touch them, still less capture them,
For one who tried would be struck down by lightning.
But if one could succeed, our powers are ended.
One thing alone can break the three goats' magic:
If they should learn to drink the blood of mortals."

Now Muji's bride told him of all of this,
And told him also that the witches' spell
Keeps her within these mountains, or she dies.
And Muji stroked his mustache, and he said:
"You'll see. Soon you will be in my serai."
He gives his carrier-pigeon to his bride,
And now he's mounted on his yearling horse,
And near-berserk, he gallops to Judbinë —
Ah, what a killer's face he had on then! —
But turned aside, and went on to his grange,
And gets up on the roof and loads his cannon,
And fires it so the whole land echoes wide.
They heard it in Judbinë and in Kraj too
And everybody gathered at his gate.
He chose from them the best three hundred men
And from the rooftop he commenced to speak:
"Fetch hunting dogs and horses, all of you.
Three wild goats there are that graze the mountain
Pastures of the Turks and infidels.
Their hair is spun out of the finest gold,
Their horns are solid bullion through and through.
If anyone mistakenly kills one of them,
I'll cut his head off, roll it down the mountain,
Because we need to take those goats alive."

And now he leads them to the distant heights;

Behind him ride the silent warriors,
And after them the packhorses and dogs.
And to the witches' mountain now they came.
When Muji reached the chosen battlefield
He gave the signal to surround the meadow,
So that the goats were cut off from the water.
Then they positioned all the dogs and horsemen,
And so a fearful massacre began.
The goats pried off the heads of fifty men,
But now the goats were thirsty, could not drink.
They slaughtered fifty more, but still the stream
Was blocked by men of Kraj and of Judbinë.
Fifty more died, but now at last the goats,
For whom their thirst was heavier than gold,
Quenched it by drinking of the blood of men.
At once the spell was broken, and with ease
He ropes the goats, ties them behind his horse,
And leads them back in triumph to Judbinë.

And soon the witches felt their power wane,
And went to find the goats from which it came;
They leap from rock to rock, from peak to peak,
Until they find their golden goats are gone.
Then a good thought comes to Muji's bride.
She sends a bird to Muji with a message
That the three witches' powers now start to curdle.
And Muji gets the news, and so at last
Meets with the three weird sisters face to face.

"For these my people you have turned to stone,
For those my own fine horses that you froze,
And for that bride that you have stolen from me,

I in return have tamed your golden goats."
The witches burn at this, but can say only:
"If you might kindly give us back our goats,
We will return your men to what they were,
Restore your horses, and give back your bride."
But Muji strokes his mustache and replies:
"I do not care a fig for men or bride,
And I cannot give back your sacred goats,
Having seen nothing half so beautiful."

Hear what the youngest witch now finds to do:
She goes down on her knees before the master,
Tears in her eyes and begging on her tongue,
Seizes his hands and puts them to her face
And prays for their return. Now, like the goats,
Muji is tamed, and lets the goats go free.
And to the eternal mountains go the witches,
Restore the goats to their high pastures green,
And then they lead the bride back to his door,
And greet him with the groomsmen and the horses,
And so the bride embraces him at last,
And the three witches get back all their powers.

But when the cup goes round, this tale is told,
The menfolk answer with a curse upon
Whoever puts his trust upon a woman.

COURTSHIP, FLIRTATION, AND LOVE

"SWEET, WHERE WERE YOU LINGERING?"

"Sweet, where were you lingering?"
"By the window, embroidering."
"If next morning is good weather,
Let's pick raspberries together."
Girl and boy, like flower and flower,
Meet within a shady bower.
Boy is happy, girl is grieving.
"Sweet, what sobs are these you're heaving?"
"Youth, good cause I have for sorrow:
I must start to pack tomorrow,
Join the caravan on the way
To the flatlands far away.
Wretched I, that must leave you —
Wretched you, what will you do
In the mountains' snow and rain,
Lonely, when will we meet again?
And the winter presses so,
Boreas begins to blow,
No-one there to make your bed,
No-one to make sure you're fed,
No-one to hold your body dear — "
"Sweetheart, sweetheart, never fear:
I will follow with my sheep,
Down into the valleys deep;
When I need you, I won't wait,
Make a cabin by your gate,
Fire my gun ten times when I
Need to have your sweet self nigh;
In the cabin, just we two,
All the world in me and you,

We will set the heights afire,
Mountains blazing higher and higher,
But our love will bring the spring,
Bring the leaf and flowering!"

"WHERE SHALL WE MEET?"

"Tell me, where's your private bower?"
"By the river, by the cherry,
Shaded by the rowanberry,
Where the scent of melon-flower
Mingles with the rose's power."
"Mrikë Paragon, give me
Those red lips and cheeks I see."
"I dare not, they've set out sentries
Guarding all my house's entries.
That's my husband's work, that jack,
May he choke till he turns black,
May a cannon crush his wick,
What I give him make him sick."
Mrikë Paragon, whose calves
Make men fall apart in halves,
To the Pasha takes her claim.
"I have not the Pasha's fame,
I am Mrs. Whatshisname—"
"Whatshisname, that piping oaf?—
Where did he get this sugar-loaf?"
"I'm a Paragon, from Shkrel."
"If I'd seen you first, know well
You'd have servants twenty-one,
And a palace of fine stone,
Softest muffins you would eat,
In our mountainside retreat.
But I couldn't leave you here—
All the town would kiss you, dear."

BEAUTY WITH A WHITE SHAWL

"Hey, beauty in your milk-white shawl,
Have those breasts budded out at all?"
"They started just a week ago,
A week, I think, maybe a year.
They've got bad habits as they grow,
They're hard, and they stick out to here.
My bodice chafes them, and they flow
With sherbet if you touch them, so."

"Now won't you give some to the squire,
Some of that sweet stuff to me?"
"I'll save it for a boy with fire,
Young, unmarried, young and free,
Someone who will rise much higher,
Who sings and plays his flute for me."

"MILLER, MILLER"

"See, miller, see!
Miller, look at me.
Make this night your special night,
Grind my wheat for me!"
"Look, pretty girl,
Sorry, pretty girl,
My grindstone's got no water,
No grinding there will be."

"See, miller, see,
Lay your eyes on me,
Isn't it a pretty sight,
And for you it's free."
"Ah, pretty girl,
What a pretty girl,
With those eyes so dark and bright
You have magicked me."

"See, miller, see,
Miller, look at me!
Let my eyes be yours tonight,
Grind my wheat for me."
"Oh, pretty girl,
Pretty, pretty girl,
You have made my grindstone sweat,
It will grind your wheat, and yet
As fine as fine can be!"

TWO BEAUTIES

Two beauties go down to the well,
One's a woman, one's a girl.
"Stop there, woman, talk to me,
Find me a bride for company,
Find me my bride of fantasy,
And I'll give my holster, see,
And my watch of filigree,
Gun with grips of ivory."
"Calm down, boy, don't be so rash,
Keep your guns and your fine trash.
I, or she you want, will meet you."
"If you're human, I entreat you,
Come together where I'll greet you —
Once is not as good as twice."
"Yes, I know you'd find that nice;
But two melons in one hand
Is more than you, young man, could stand,
Hand can't cut and knife can't sever,
Squeezed between us you would shiver
Seven years in quartain fever,
And there is no doctor ever
Who could cure that foolish lover."
"If it's written I must die,
In your laps then let me lie,
Let your little mouths be speaking
Poetry for our leave-taking,
And your black eyes weeping, aching,
While your white hands close my eyes —
And, though dead, I would arise!"

BEAUTY AT THE DOOR

"Beauty, beauty, at your door,
Make me happy one time, or
I will curse you twelve times more:
May your oxen die in spring,
May your land lack managing,
May your man be quarrelling,
May your cow die while you're milking,
May your sheep die while you're shearing,
May your guard dog die a-barking,
And your lambs a-gamboling,
Calves while drinking at the spring,
May your horse die cantering,
And your house burn down in Fall,
If you won't give me your all,
May God cripple you withal;
Ease me not while I am young,
May God pull out your eyes and tongue."
"Little sparrow, little fellow,
May your God send you to Hell-O."

SUNG ACROSS THE SHOULDER:

"HEY, GIRL"

"Give me a glance of that bright eye!
Or may your lusts be crushed and die,
May fevers catch you in the spring,
No health may winter, summer bring;
Give me that eye, or may your friend
Come to a miserable end,
Your attic cock choke in mid-crow,
Your oxen die before the plow;
Give me a touch of that white neck,
Or may your fields all turn to rock,
Your house a flooded meadow where
Folk come to fill their buckets there;
Give me that neck, or truly may
Wasting sickness bear you away
(Despite what doctors do or say):
And for a mattress you'll have hay,
And for a quilt, dry holly-leaves,
And your soul wail with liars and thieves."

"You bold young bastard, what's this prattle?
I'm ready if you want a battle;
Let's fight, and wrestle for a fall,
And even if you win the brawl,
You will cry uncle, never fear.
But if you get a hold down here,
There's babyfat so fresh and nice,
You never dreamed such paradise;
And then, my boy, you'll bless the one
Who bore you, making you a man."

"HEY, BEAUTIFUL!"

"Beauty by the flowerbed,
Head up like a thoroughbred,
Hear what I have got to say:
If I catch you, caught you'll stay.

I have got a heavy jones,
I've a yen to jump your bones,
Pink cheeks, breasts as white as snow,
Two big handfuls, just like so,
Damned if I will let them go!"
"Suck my white tits, young Sir Randy?
You'd go crazy, like they're brandy,
Kill somebody, like enough,
Then go home to sleep it off."

"I'd kill twenty, literally,
Just to lie upon your belly —
Where'd you get those cheeks I see?"
"Almighty God gave them to me,
Given me by God Almighty:
Partly fat and partly meaty,
Partly muscle, partly fatty,
Just to please my latest sweetie,
Just to keep my lover happy —
But he must be young and peppy,
So that when I hear his call,
I will let my dinner fall,
I will leave my own grave-dust
To be the roadmap of his chest —
But I hope we will both die

On the same night, you and I;
And we'll lie there, grave by grave—
Who needs Heaven if you've love?"

MARRIAGE SONGS

TO THE BRIDE

Bridey, bridey, sweet and coy,
Mount the pony,
Bear a boy,
Name him Paladin, for joy.
Like the paladin of Hoti,
To God's vow he'll be devoted;
Like the paladin of Grudë,
He'll be brave and wise and good;
Like the paladin of Kelmend,
Harvest legends without end;
Like the paladin of Kastrat,
You'll find nobody like that;
Like the paladin of Shkrel,
Trickier than sprites from Hell!

THE COCK AND THE BRIDE

Milorad of Montenegro
And a girl from Sarajevo
Were in marriage to be tied:
Lovely Etleva, the bride.
But she loved another man:
Gjergji the Albanian.
He had sworn upon his life
He would have no other wife.
There was endless bitter strife,
Loaded musket, whetted knife.
Both sides reached agreement then,
To take it to the wise old men.
Alban, Montenegrin sages
Gathered, seasoned by the ages;
It was given them to decide
Who should best deserve the bride.
Old man Kasel, that wise fox,
Said "It can be solved with cocks.
Go, young men--and heed my words—
Home and fetch your fighting birds.
He whose cock will win the fight
Gets the girl as his by right."
Milos' cock was speckled gray,
Gjergji's red and black, they say.
They fight cruelly, eye to eye,
Head to head, to kill or die.
Red-and-black will win the fight;
Gjergji gets the girl that night.

SHE WHISPERS TO HER LOVER

"So many groomsmen, what a to-do!"
"I hope they brought some singers too."
"They'll make me sing, but what I'll do
Is sing and dance, my love, for you."
They start the feasting right away,
Three whole sets the band must play
Until "it's time for bed!" they say.
"Three years he hasn't shaved, the clown.
The filthy beggar tickles me,
His hand creeps up upon my knee,
He tries a love-bite then, the swine—
I kicked him where the sun don't shine.
He cracked his head on the chiffonniers,
But now his mother overhears.
That black bride, what is she doing?—
I paid three thousand for her wooing.
It's almost day, and now she's moaning,
Says she's sick, can't move for groaning—
So I say "Come sit by the fire
Where the light's a little higher,
Let me read your rosary.
If my bride should die, why, we
Are ruined, house and family."
She drags me by my amulet
To the hearth where fire is set.
"Wake up, Hajj, read her beads for me,
Lest she die and ruin me!"
"Wake up yourself, any fool can see
Without the beads just why she moans.
Lust has got into her bones,

White face, black eyes, how she yearns;
It is for a boy she burns."
May the Hajj catch all diseases,
Let him be whom our sickness seizes!
What he wants is what I've got,
And he'll surely get it—not!

POOR HYSEN

Creditors have all come calling,
He's sold his goats, both kids and dams;
He's sold his cows, their calves a-bawling,
He's sold his sheep, he's sold their lambs:
There's nothing left, unless he'd rather
Sell his mother and his father.
He'll avenge this bloody spending;
Indeed he will, and no pretending:
"Right. I'm going to the market."
When he got into the market
He put the word out far and wide:
He is there to sell his bride.
There he meets a smart young dandy
Seems to find the offer handy:
"What's the price for her, my man?"
— Words that cut as word well can.
"My wife will cost three hundred ducats."
Hand goes quickly to his pockets,
Finds in there three hundred ducats,
Gets his bride and home he goes.
What grand wedding now he throws!
But when bed-time came, and they
Touched each other's flesh, the sky
Curdled in a bloody whey
With the frown of God above.
To the window flew a dove:
Told him "All these signs of doom
Pale before what is to come:
Your own mother bore your bride."
Twice the young man died inside;

Now to comfort him, she tried
Questioning him of his mother:
"Poor man, did you have a sister?"
"Wretched girl, had you a brother?"
"I left behind a little brother
With a birthmark like a blister
On his forehead, from his mother."
Lightning-fast, he fetched a light,
Raised his cap to show the sight:
There the mark was, red and white.
So embracing, they begin
To weep the fate that made them kin.

MARTA GOSSIPS

Marta tells the girls that please her:
"Poor wife saddled with a geezer.
Daddy wed me to this oldie,
Buried me alive with Moldy.
Nothing's worse than when you face
Death's-head by the fireplace.
Sixty years went to create
Gray-bush beard and barren pate.
Drool is all he gives, or worse:
Daddy, here's a daughter's curse."

SPELLS, CHARMS, AND GAMES

A CHARM AGAINST SNAKEBITE

Gospod Pusi called a wedding,
So he sent for Gospod Peri:
"Hold this wedding ceremony,
Let there be no wicked bride,
Let there be a virtuous bride,
May the snake die of her beauty,
May her goodness heal the sting."

SONG OF THE SALT

(A divination ritual, in which the diviner sprinkles salt on his palm, then takes two hairs from his client's head, crosses them over the salt, and then places over them a coin taken at random by the client from his pocket (which will be the diviner's fee). The diviner then squeezes his hand, blows on the contents, and reads the shapes suggested by the salt. The "whoo" sound in the poem represents the blowing.)

Whoo, whoo, black bear,
Whoo, whoo, white bear.
Whoo, spellbinder,
Earthborn pixie,
Water-nixie,
May the weak mind
And the strong mind
Melt in songlines,
Where is healing,
There is fortune.
Whoo, whoo, whoo!

112

CURING A BUNION

North wind blow and crack the sky,
What was seen be seen no more;
White shades chase the gods on high,
Blistered are their heels so sore,
Gods' hands now as feet must tread —
Where has all the gods' power fled?
In between the warp-threads that
Rule the fabric of the mat
That was pulled by evil hate
From beneath your proper fate.
Dark northwind blow sky to ice,
Gods for you make sacrifice;
Hands are hands now, and not feet,
Feet, not hands, now serve as feet.
Now the gods' powers are a knife
Cutting out the bunion's life,
Digging out the evil eyes,
So they cannot see to rise.

HOST AND GUEST

(an "Icicle Song," improvised response poem)

HOST:
Welcome friends and god-kin dear,
I rejoice that you are here;
Take your merry ease tonight,
No scale will measure our delight.

GUEST:
Icicle song in its first pressing:
Honor to you, our host, and blessing,
Never may your table cease
To flow with gifts, soul of Malësisë.

HOST:
I saved the grape of the southward hill,
And brewed it in my finest still,
Aged it, drew it, for cordial good,
From the cask of mulberry wood.

GUEST:
You always had the ancient grace
To nurture noble words and ways,
Gave your guests kindly courtesy:
God grant your fields fertility!

HAT SONG

(an "Icicle Song," improvised by the winning team to the losers of the Hat Game)

At start of play when down I sat
Among ten hats I hid my nut;
You picked the first and picked in vain,
Picked up the second — wrong again.

To seek a nut's too deep for you:
Acorns are all you ever knew;
You rummage barren leaves but find
Nothing, with your toplofty mind.

One hundred points, and now it's two:
What kind of hobgoblins are you?
You'll never win by guessing it:
So may your hands turn all to shit!

HYMNS AND RITUALS

THE BIRTHDAY OF SAINT NICHOLAS

Wise and learned this fair morn,
Here Saint Nicholas was born:
Three weeks nothing, day and night,
Passed his lips, poor little wight,
Since at mother's breast he fed:
Mother, father, both are dead.
All their flocks and goods remain:
Who will keep them for him then?

They'll be guarded by the poor:
All who rise at dawn footsore,
Toil to earn a bite for pay
Go to church this holy day,
Where they will rejoice, because
They're blessing baby Santa Claus.

Who is he, we do not know,
That he should on us bestow
All his riches and his treasure,
Ark of blessings beyond measure,
That's inscribed with: FOR THE POOR:
May God bless him always, for
He is the fair saint of light.

But we are in such a plight!
Wilting as the lily will,
Weeping willow on the rill,
Bending as the willow arches,
Overwhelmed with so much riches.

It's too much for us, although
We're the poorest folk we know;
We'll just leave the rich ark be,
So that one more poor than we
In worldly goods or holy spirit
May its sacred wealth inherit—
And that our Saint Nicholas,
Saint of light, remain with us.

Amen.

THE BLESSED VIRGIN

Mary comes to our relief,
In her arms an olive-sheaf;
Heaven's eyelids open, where
Every olive is a star.
Night and day, our souls to save,
Jesus quakes all through his cave;
Now the stars fall from their height,
Village turns to city bright—
What to do with all this light?
On the offshoot the bulbul sings:
Sleep, if you can't hear these things.
Are you of the day or night?
Choose the darkness or the light.

TO THE CHRISTIAN PRIEST

You, the Christian priest,
Are being called by old graves,
Those old graves
Among which lie also our Albanians.

Give your blessing to everybody
But also to those old Albanians;
Let everybody hear your blessing,
Because we all respect the Mother of God.

LAMENT FOR PRENG GRUDA

Preng, son of Gjon, what grief is here?
What a crowd attends your bier?
HEIA!
Mountain birds ask shriekingly:
Lord, what is this tragedy?
HEIA!
Gruda's son in exile dead,
This day dawned with him, and fled;
Now his line is waste and blind,
No son or daughter left behind.
HEIA!

But he leaves his history,
Spread Albania far and free;
Malësisë' great ones on this day
Mourn Preng Gruda, passed away;
All night within these frontiers grieve
Those to whom his help he gave,
None here passed a night unless
He had helped them in distress.
HEIA!

Every child that God gives here,
When he's reached his thirteenth year,
Left his crib, and learned to speak,
Then his father he will seek,
Asks permission if he may
Into exile pass away.
Friendless in the world he'd roam:
With Preng Gruda found a home,

Food, and fire, and honor found,
Someone in a far cold land
Who could hear their voice and tongue,
Homesick, struggling, and young.
No-one, Preng, you turned away,
All who knocked your door could stay,
You would never hide nor shun,
But were friend to everyone.
HEIA!

Education was your rule,
All your kin must go to school;
All Malësisë has felt your aid,
For you loved your Tring and Dedë,
Dearly loved your Kol and Gjokë,
Though far, would not forget your folk:
See these Albanians from Detroit
Come back to mourn you at your feet.
HEIA!

Black blazes there the house of stone;
Who takes the dark gift? God alone.
God made men worthy of their death:
The bird that is the spirit's breath
Has flown away from its last home,
Beats with its wings the winds of fame.
For he was born a great-souled one,
A writer, scholar, muses'-son,
And knew to question us, that we
Might learn to judge as well as he.
HEIA!

O Preng, may then the good muse bless
Your written words with deathlessness,
That what you wrote outlast the page,
For words set out before the age
Of paper, and will come to land
Beyond it, as my lines now stand.
HEIA!

God held us once, and always will;
May you, your words, remain so still
With Him, as these great mountains will.

HAI! HEIA!

PHILOSOPHY

LET YOUR WORK BE WELL OR ILL...

Let your work be well or ill,
Criticisms will assail it:
Expectation's cruel knell,
Words as sharp as knives will hail it.

Since this life was first devised,
Though it last without an ending,
Whose work was not criticized,
All its beauty notwithstanding?

In each human heart there wakes
Swiftly that innate reaction:
Even God's sky shrinks and shakes,
Pelted from each new direction.

Joined at birth with mortal man
Comes ambition's desert spirit:
If you have it, no-one can
Rest until the burial pit.

Criticism when it grows
Limp, unfounded, like the grasses,
Shatters the morale of those
Who inspire our human masses.

Critics, like the ocean wave,
Should not damage one's aspiring —
Thus the truly strong and brave
Work despite them, still untiring.

If you'd be life's critic true,
Beauty's deep roots you must find:
Otherwise your rantings do
But throw pebbles at the wind.

WHAT IS WITHIN A MAN

Mountain peak with forests high,
Over them a star-filled sky.
Sky's belly and the high peaks clear
Clasp a space, an empty sphere,
Where, between, in bubble form,
Songs are pricked, and burst in storm,
Sound now like a rushing flume,
Now like terror's frozen tomb,
Now, love's melody that plays
Over the ribcage of the days;
And this warm breath, like a steam,
Fills the sphere with hope and dream.
So of God the inner man
Prays to be remade again,
Asks that He come down to earth,
Give our mothers second birth;
Without You, we're men with wings,
Frozen midair, like unborn things.

AFTERWORD

ALBANIAN ORAL POETRY AS A GIFT EXCHANGE

By Gjekë MARINAJ

THE PROJECT

After a medical emergency prevented the American poet Frederick Turner from accompanying me into some of the unpublished and unrecorded labyrinths of Albanian epic poetry, I found myself taking the trip and conducting the research on my own. However, knowing that Turner would continue to work with me throughout the project as soon as I returned to The University of Texas at Dallas, where this idea initially started, I anxiously finished the research within the preplanned time frame. Oral epic poetry, I must confess, had never been my favorite segment of the body of literature. But after the initial experience of doing what really amounted to ethnography, I simply changed my mind. As a poet, I found myself profoundly excited, and without knowing it, I was thrown into a situation where I was being an anthropologist and an ethnographer as well. Instead of dealing with abstract oral-literary issues, I was dealing with a whole culture that resonated with my own earlier life.

It was at UTD that I become excited with the study of traditional and ancient oral literature. When I returned to Albania, that interest linked up with my childhood experiences. I found in Albania something very interesting and of much value today, which was very moving to me as a poet. My old

135

memories came back, and I realized that in spite of everything I was still an Albanian mountaineer and an Albanian poet, and all that came back to me. I realized that Malësia e Madhe, known as the epicenter of Albanian epic songs, was still my center of gravity as a poet, as a human being.

There was a certain kind of poetic irony in the trip itself: in some strange way through that period I, fortunately, was silenced by losing my voice. Luckily for me, people thought it was actually laryngitis, and they did not question me about it. Whatever it was, to me there was something very symbolic about it. In some way, my own voice as a poet had to be suppressed for a while, in order for me to be able to hear these ancient songs coming from my feisty, wonderful, humorous, proud people.

This book is meant to offer the English-language reader only a small part of Albanian oral poetry. What we humbly offer here is truly essential to Albanian literature and culture, because there is no identity of a people more synonymous with the strength, spirit, and beauty of their own epic songs than that of the Albanians. The Albanian language, it has been argued, is the true distinction of the Albanian people. But it is their historic, legendary, and other lyric folk songs that have kept the language alive throughout their rich and complex history.

This is, in part, what actually made us dedicate so much time and effort to the translation of these proto-epic oral poems into English. Oral epic poetry, we believe, is not only poetry in its own right, but the root code of language itself. And true translation must continue and honor that process of language-making. "[T]his is even more important than a knowledge of the source language: a poet can make himself into some kind of scholar — or, failing that, can work with a scholar — but a scholar cannot make himself into any kind of poet if he is not one already" (Kussi, Bosley, and Branch, 17).

THE SURVIVAL OF ALBANIAN POETRY AND LANGUAGE

Actually, the worst thing that ever happened to the epic poetry of the Balkans was its division into racial groups. Epic poetry is better explained and understood in linguistic terms. The Albanian language is itself distinct, with its own history. It has an integrity that is as unique as most recognized branches of the other Indo-European languages. There is no question among linguists about that. Poetry is language and language is poetry. What keeps languages alive is precisely the poets.

It has always been that way. Languages die, in part, because they do not have a great tradition of poetry in them. If it has a great tradition of poetry in it, the language will stay alive even if the language is spoken by people who have very little trace of biological, racial, or ethnic connection to a particular geographical area. Language holds a very powerful role in the betterment of a nation's life, and when it is infused with the art of poetry, it can do cultural wonders, regardless of its geographical boundaries. Here is a good example, not from Albanian literature and culture, but from the history of Czech literature:

When Czech literature emerges into the full light of day, we find not primitive beginnings, but a highly developed literary situation in which Czech poets and scholars, accustomed to write in the international languages of church and state, to an increasing extent began to compose in their native tongue, bringing it to a cultural maturity that was the product of a long literary tradition. (Matejka, Mersereau, and Welsh, 19)

Much the same could be said of Albanian literature. For

thousands of years, in "the land of the eagles," as Albanians have nicknamed their country, the songs of the *lahuta* (a single-stringed instrument) have played a unique moral and physiological role. The lines taken from "Homage to the Warriors" clearly illustrate that:

> When I take my lute to sing
> Snow-peaks perch upon my string,
> And the forest heights fall still
> And the starry heavens chill
> And the ice-fields and the crests
> Come to sing the heroes' gests.
> Words like water from the spring
> Teach the heroes' deeds to sing;
> Green-clad hillsides raise the call
> Echoed from the mountain-wall.

They also show the reasoning of the people of Malësia e Madhe when they claim that their epic poems, këngët Kreshnike (the Kreshinik songs), "make men stronger, braver; give courage to endure the bullet, the blood, the wars where the men are lost" (Sako and Haxhihasani, 10).

WHO ARE THE ALBANIANS?

This question is important because the whole notion of national identity with respect to their neighboring countries is a relatively new issue for Albania and its people. Regardless of their embryonic origin, they found themselves in Illyria, and Illyria is what they called their homeland. If foreigners knocked on their doors and the reasons of their visit were pleasure, they did the best they could to entertain them as guests. If they were there for business, they made their goods, ports, and seashores available to them. If they came to occupy their land or kick them out of their own territory, they built gigantic castles like that of Rozafat, an Illyrian fortification, and fought with everything in their possession to never have to resettle elsewhere. Even when they had no alphabet—though as early as 1689 Albanian historians discovered a letter "written in the old northern alphabet" (Shuteriqi, 5)—they had their language and their epic songs, two important components that made them feel comfortable as a distinct Illyrian people.

Even as the transition from calling themselves Illyrians to being self-identified as Albanians took place, they protected their language, poetry, and territory without feeling the need to prove their national identity to anyone. In 1389, when the Battle of Kosovo started, they had no compunction about joining the Serbs and other nations to create a coalition of Balkan forces, and fought against the Ottoman Sultan Murat I. Their contented taking for granted of their identity led some Albanian writers like Marin Barleti (1450–1520) to utilize a defensive tone:

> There might be people who will tell me that: These are old issues. I know that as well, but the older they are the more divine they appear to be: all these great merits gain dignity, importance, and authority, and, if you will, some kind of religious honor analogous to the elderly who day in and day out keep getting older, and we honor them at the same rate, which is in contrast with our contemporaries; although our love toward them seems to be sweeter, we somehow tend to respect them less; similarly, the old good deeds hold more importance then the new ones even though the newer they are the sweeter they are. (Barleti, 149)

If the truth be told, it was a number of prominent non-Albanians, among them William Shakespeare, Lord Byron, and British traveler-writer Mary Edith Durham, who did the work of identification for them. In Act I, scene ii of Shakespeare's comedy *Twelfth Night* or *What You Will* (written between 1600 and 1602 and published in 1623), the heroine Viola asks a captain and a small group of sailors: "What country, friends, is this?" and the captain responds "This is Illyria, lady." Viola asks again: "And what should I do in Illyria?" And the action of the play thenceforth is set in that real but also imaginary country.

Lord Byron's letter to his mother sent from Prevesa on November 12, 1809, and his excitement about meeting with Albanian people and their leader Ali Pasha Tepelena (1740–1822) have proved to be important to the Albanians and interesting to the other parts of the world. Here is the first paragraph of the letter:

My dear Mother,

I have now been some time in Turkey. The place is on the coast but I have traversed the interior of the province of Albania on a visit to the Pacha. I left Malta in the Spider, a brig of war, on the 21st of September and arrived in eight days at Prevesa. I thence have been about 150 miles as far as Tepaleen, his highness' country palace, where I staid three days. The name of the Pacha is Ali, and he is considered a man of the first abilities, he governs the whole of Albania (the ancient Illyricum), Epirus and part of Macedonia. His son Velly Pacha, to whom he has given me letters, governs the Morea and he has great influence in Egypt, in short he is one of the most powerful men in the Ottoman empire. When I reached Yanina the capital after a journey of three days over the mountains through country of the most picturesque

140

beauty, I found that Ali Pacha was with his army in Illyricum besieging Ibraham Pacha in the castle of Berat. He had heard that an Englishman of rank was in his dominion and had left orders in Yanina with the Commandant to provide a house and supply me with every kind of necessary, gratis, and though I have been allowed to make presents to the slaves etc. I have not been permitted to pay for a single article of household consumption. I rode out on the vizier's horses and saw the palaces of himself and grandsons; they are splendid but too much ornamented with silk and gold. I then went over the mountains through Zitza, a village with a Greek monastery (where I slept on my return) in the most beautiful situation (always excepting Cintra in Portugal) I ever beheld. In nine days I reached Tepaleen, our journey was much prolonged by the torrents that had fallen from the mountains and intersected the roads. I shall never forget the singular scene on entering Tepaleen at five in the afternoon as the sun was going down, it brought to my recollection (with some change of dress however) Scott's description of Branksome Castle in his lay, and the feudal system. (See www. albanianliterature.com)

Edith Durham's metaphoric comment is famous: "Empires came and went, and passed over the Albanian as does water off a duck's back" (Durham, 4). She describes the folk of that region as "A fierce tribal people, known as Illyrians," who "in about 300 B.C. were invaded by the Celts, who have probably left a deep mark on the people of to-day by the infusion of Celtic blood" (Durham, 2). Her book High Albania is one of the most frequently referenced books on the topic of Albanian identity. Many other photographers, anthropologists, ethnographers, historians, and traveling writers, of course, expressed similar thoughts, for all of which the Albanian people were and remain grateful.

But all that research, professional determination, and human kindness started to backfire, not only on them as authors but also on the Albanian people and their ancient history. From the first decades of the twentieth century to the present day, regardless of the voluminous new findings of contemporary scholarship, the debate over Albanian identity still seems to bounce from one extreme to the other. Some Albanian scholars, clerics, and historians insist (without mentioning a single specific Serbian name) that a number of Serbian scholars, who seem to be irritated by the whole notion of the debate, have argued against all the above. According to them, the link that connects the modern Albanians with the Illyrians is simply a myth cleverly created by the Albanians themselves in order to establish ethnic and territorial priority. Some go even further, suggesting that the Albanians either are a race of Slavic origins or are Turks who have decided to stay after numerous Ottoman wars against the Balkan nations. Reading between the lines here, assuming these are indeed comments made by Serbs, it is not the Albanian people they have a problem with, because they are willing to consider that as part of their blood, but the fact that they consider themselves to be Illyrians.

That skepticism, as might be expected, never received acceptance, either by Albanian scholars or by international ones for that matter. The debate went on and to a degree still goes on, in three main directions. First and foremost, specific topographic names in Albanian considered as distinctly Illyrian were required as evidence. Second, the origin of the Albanian language has been questioned on the basis that most ancient people have a well-known, or relatively known, ancient language. The third demand of the critics calls for a close examination of the history of Albanian literature. (At least literature is recognized by the debaters as an integral part of a people's identity.) The response of Albanian law has been to protect the language and literature as the most essential aspects of Albanian identity.

Some place the Illyrians, in the territory of modern Albania, as the first human population that ever existed in Europe:

> Thousands of years before the birth of Christ, when the Slavic tribes began their first westward stirrings, they presumably bore within their memory the patterned narratives or the formulaic verbalization to which the earliest poetry of the Balkan peoples might be traced. The first Slavs recognized in the west established a habitat in the region between the Vistula and Dnieper Rivers with the Avars, a migrant central Asian people, settled among them. Together the two began to migrate south and west into the Pannonian plain, and there they were joined by other Slavic tribes, among them the Sorbs (or "Serbs"). (Karadzic, 13)

Other scholars insist that amid the Paleolithic period is the best place to look for Albanian origins, but they give no specific topography as reference. Antonello Biagini, the author of *The History of Albanian: From the Beginning to the Present*, who also teaches Eastern European history at La Sapienza University in Rome, suggests that we should concentrate on this subject by considering two distinct assumptions: the first hypothesis is the Slavic origin of the people of the Balkans in general and of the Illyrian territory in particular (as, for instance, people who came from Western Poland); the second hypothesis confirms their Balkan autochthony (Biagini, 13). According to Albanian and foreign historians and anthropologists, including Father Zef Valentini, some tribes of Malësia e Madhe, including that of Shkrel, came from the upper Balkan mountains, including Bosnia and Novi Pazer (a city located in Serbia, in the Raška dstrict), as nomadic graziers during the early Middle Ages and settled first in Pulat and then spread out elsewhere in Malësia e Madhe. Yet the claims of Father Valentini and others who think like him, argues Dom Nikë Ukgjini, himself an important contemporary Catholic figure and writer, "should never be interpreted, as some Serb authors think, as meaning the tribes of Malësia e Madhe, such as Hoti, Kelmendi, Kastrati, and Gruda, had come from the northern areas of Bosnia during the eleventh and twelfth century and got Albanianized in these areas after their arrival" (Ukgjini, 19).

As we know now, the Albanian language is a distinct branch of the Indo-European languages: "It [Illyria] is the least-known and most interesting part of the Balkan Peninsula. The people speak a language alleged to be more ancient than Greek" (Cozens-Hardi, 401). The prominent Albanian scholar Dhimitër Shuteriqi states:

> In its embryonic stages the written Albanian language appeared mainly in private letter correspondences, in the official religious acts, and especially in the business-related documents used by a considerable number of people. Side notes of Buzuku's Missal show that the written Albanian language was used only in a few religious books. The full alphabet, handwritten by someone as a side note on one of the pages of the book, which is different from the one used by Buzuku, is an indication that more than one alphabet might have existed at that time, which proves a nonsporadic use of the language. (Shuteriqi, 4).

As British contemporary scholar Noel Malcolm eloquently explains below, there was also a short-lived challenging hypothesis that the Albanians could be identified with the people of the Caucasus area, and therefore the Albanian

144

language might be Caucasian as well:

> This Caucasian theory was first expounded by Renaissance humanists (such as Aeneas Silvius Piccolomini) who were familiar with the works of the classical geographers and historians; it was developed in the 1820s by the French diplomat and influential writer on the Balkans François Pouqueville; and in 1855 it was presented in a polemical response to the work of Johann Georg von Hahn by a Greek doctoral student at Göttingen, Nikolaos Nikokles. By the late nineteenth century this theory was in retreat, thanks to the work of linguists who had demonstrated that Albanian was definitely Indo-European, not Caucasian. One last attempt to salvage the theory, however, was made by an Arberësh writer, Francesco Tajani, who suggested that the Ur-Albanians were Scythians who spoke an Indian language but whose place of residence, before they moved to Albania, was in the Caucasus. With delightful ingenuity, Tajani derived the word shqiptar (Albanian) from the Sanskrit kship, meaning "to fight," and tar, meaning "bow" — thus demonstrating, to his own satisfaction at least, that the original Albanians were Scythian archers. (Malcolm, 75)

Things have gotten so intense that, even today, poets and writers who happen to make comments on the Balkan languages and literature feel they must apologize to the reader, because no matter how objective and neutral their intentions might be, they know that it is almost impossible to make a comment of this nature that is acceptable to all Balkan readers. To illustrate this, I am offering the following passage taken from the preface by Milne Holton and Vasa D. Mihailovich to the collected poems of the Serbian linguist and song collector Vuk Stefanović Karadžić (1787–1864), Songs of the Serbian People, published by the University of Pittsburgh Press in 1997:

> In following the tradition of identifying our subject as "Serbian," we have certainly not desired to feed the flames of ethnic divisiveness that have so long ravaged the historical experience of the South Slavs. We are fully aware that the Croats, the Bosnians, the Macedonians, and the Bulgarians lay legitimate claim to their share of this body of poetry and to the history it embodies. We have called the poems "Serbian" in reference to a nation and its language, never to any modern state, yet we have done so in full recognition of the complex nature of the literary identity that existed in the minds of the collector and the singers whose work we present here. (Karadzic, xi)

Questions about the Albanian language and literature are perfectly valid, but they always seem to generate more questions than answers. The ongoing debate wants answers for questions like: How do we place Albanian literature? In what category do we place it? It is not part of Greek literature, with which we are very familiar; equally clearly, it is not part of Slavic literature. We know that Albanian is the only language that belongs to the Illyric branch, just like the Thracian branch, which is also represented by a single modern language, the Armenian. The Albanians know about the Celtic, Germanic, Latin, Slavic, Hellenic, Iranian, Indic, and the Tokharian branches, but in terms of literary production, the rest of the world knows very little about the Illyric/Albanian branch. This is important and relevant to the topic at hand, because it is a distinct strain of the Indo-European expansion and therefore a strong source of Albanian identity.

Albanian scholars fully understood this language-literature concept. In an attempt to once again enjoy the peace of the earlier days in terms of Albanian identity, many of them, in addition to writing their own articles and academic essays, turned to the works of foreign scholars for help. Foreign writers were quoted on almost anything and everything they had to say about Albanian culture. The German historian Franz Altheim (1898–1976), who also studied philology, archaeology, and linguistics and lectured on these subjects at the University of Frankfurt, at the University of Halle, and the University of Berlin, was one of the people who were quoted frequently. He not only supported the idea that the Albanians are full-blooded Illyrians, but went even further, saying that "Towards the end of the thirteenth century B.C., the Illyrians earned for the first time an important place in world history" (Sapthari, 250).

Canadian-born Robert Elsie is another Albanian scholar, who has earned the love and the respect of Albanian society in and outside of the country for his undisputed efforts to keep Albanian literature on the map of world literature. As a distinguished translator and scholar Elsie has provided more specific evidence on behalf of the Albanian identity than arguably any non-Albanian ever has. Objective claims like the following: "The setting of the 'Songs of the Frontier Warriors' within the context of seventeenth-century border skirmishes during the Austro-Turkish wars perhaps constitutes, for its part, simply the crystallized literary form of much earlier Balkan legendry, predating the arrival of the Slavs" (Elsie, 182–83) have had more effect on international opinion regarding this issue than all the government catalogs during the regime of Enver Hoxha combined. I am not arguing here that all government-produced folkloric catalogs were worthless, but the propagandistic spin they utilized often sounded something like this: "The classics tell us of the ancient Illyrians, of their renowned war songs and their skillful playing on the flute, of their dances such as

147

pyrrhike, which was famous in ancient times, and such Illyrian costumes as Dalmatica, which were to spread throughout the ancient world in the first century A.D." (Zojsi, Dojaka, and Qatipi, 2). By contrast, the evidence Elsie provides to support his arguments is concrete and appropriately chosen.

ON THE ANTIQUITY OF THE ILLYRIAN ORAL TRADITION

A few years back, after a valuable tip from a Chinese restaurant owner who remembered his father talking about an old Albanian poem published in a Chinese journal that was published in the United States in the late twenties, I started to narrow down the Chinese publications published in America from the 1920s to the 1950s. Only quite recently, however, with the kind assistance of Mary Yeh, Ph.D., was I able to locate the journal. I found the poem titled "The Son of King Bardhyl" in a Literary Supplement Pamphlet placed in the Literature and Art Section of the *China Journal*. The poem was translated from the Chinese into English in 1891 by Arthur Sowerby, who was probably the father of the editor of the journal, Arthur de Carle Sowerby (1885–1954). Even though I will not rest until I find the Chinese version of the poem (ideally translated into Chinese in a bilingual edition), I have to be satisfied meanwhile that this four-line stanza poem exists at all. For now, all I can do is make an educated presumption that the poem must have been translated into Chinese sometime between 206 B.C.E. and 220 C.E. during the Han Dynasty. King Bardyl(lis) ruled Dardania from 385 to 358 B.C. Here is the song:

> Ho Malësi, po t'shtrej fjalë për maja brryli;
> Sot asht shtua me djal kral Bardhyli.

148

Illiri ynë Klintu emnin djalit ja ka than
Na u baft për shpatë, e na u baft për nam!

— Përkthyer nga Kinezçja
Nga Arthur Sowerby, 1891

Ho Malci, across the elbow words I lay;
King Bardhyli(s) had his son today,
Klintu our Illyrian has named his son
May he be a swordsman, a famous one!

— Translated from the Chinese by
Arthur Sowerby, 1891 (Sowerby, 288–89 pmf.)

Nevertheless, based on the language, content, and structure of the poem, we have every reason to believe that this stanza is a song (or part of a song) that belongs to the "Sung Across the Shoulder" genre. We can compare it stylistically with the following lines taken from a more recent song of this nature, itself titled "Sung Across the Shoulder":

Hark to what the grapevine cries:
Tells Gjokova to arise,
Calls across the west wind's bluster:
Peja and Rugovë to muster!
Here's a hint from one who knows:
Troopship landing many foes,
Pouring out as black as crows.

The ancient poem is in the authentic Albanian meter and form; in only four lines we find more information about the Illyrians than in hundreds of speculating essays combined. That is the true power of the epic verse.

When a poem is truly historical and has no relation to political manipulation it can survive cultural, linguistic, stylistic, and, above all, historical changes and still keep the historical facts straight. From this point of view, I agree with Starve Th. Frasheri's comment on the epic verse that "a song not only changes in content, but travels as well from one place to another. Each place alters the song in accordance with its own character, and this very fact makes it difficult to trace its origin" (Frasheri, 88).

Nevertheless, the context is the poetic power of Albanian historic epic poetry. The fact that we have these few fragments that come to us from very, very long ago clearly indicates that there was a vital literary tradition going on in 300 B.C. and that this has been continuous. The "Songs Across the Shoulder" are still being performed in current oral poetry, and that particular idiom goes back to 300 B.C.

BALKAN VIOLENCE AND THE ROLE OF THE POETS

As Durham has so intuitively detected, "It is the fashion among journalists and others to talk of the 'lawless Albanians'; but there is perhaps no other people in Europe so much under the tyranny of laws" (Durham, 41). In many ways, this holds true even today in Malësia e Madhe because, as Leonard Fax noticed, "Albanian customary law has left its mark on the character of the people, a fact confirmed by their moral and ethical standards, such as a sense of honor, vengefulness, courage and decisiveness in critical situations, and a feeling of closeness within the family, the brotherhood, and the clan" (Canuni, Camaj, xiv).

But the role of poets in preserving these unwritten laws can

150

be open to serious charges. Sadly, according to a 1894 report published in the *Geographical Journal*, these kinds of customary laws have had devastating results "in a country like Northern Albania, where not seventy-five percent of the people die a natural death" (Cozens-Hardy). Many of the poems translated here reflect the circumstances under which such enormous human losses could be tolerated.

Most contemporary scholars agree that territorial conflicts have contributed to this way of life at least as much as the art of the oral poetry. Indeed, it could be argued that the poets were, if anything, international and nonpartisan in their sympathies. Milman Parry and Albert Lord in the mid-1930s dedicated a great deal of time and effort trying to determine the major poets of the Slavic part of the Balkan states, their ethnicity, and above all the nature of their concerns in their respective heroic epic songs. And "interestingly enough, four out of the five singers whose songs appear in this [their] volume were Albanians: Salih Ugljanin, Djemal Zogic, Sulejman Makic and Alija Fjuljanin. These singers from Novi Pazar in the Sanjak were willing and able to reproduce the same epic songs in Bosnian (Serbo-Croatian) and Albanian" (Elsie and Mathie-Heck, v). This statement attests to the fact that epic poets are not only innocent of stirring up ethnic conflicts but should actually be credited for their efforts to minimize the importance of ethnic and geographical divisions, as well as for emphasizing that epic poetry is an art of all the people of the Balkans. In other words, if four out of five poets that Parry and Lord studied in the Slavic Balkans were Albanians, then Hardy's statistics on Albanian deaths outside of natural causes cannot be blamed on the epic poets but rather on the nature of the social structure of the Balkans. This could mean that the people of Malësia e Madhe should look within their own and their neighbors' social and political spheres to find answers that would explain the reasoning for their historically inexhaustible deadly conflicts with the Montenegrins, Serbs, and Bosnians.

Did they really hate their neighbors—and vice versa—that much? Did they blame the conflicts on the epic poets and oral poetry? These questions were on the tip of my tongue everywhere I went during my trip to Albania. I knew that now we could begin to explore this other organic branch of Indo-European culture. And I will never forget a passage that the Albanian dictator Enver Hoxha used to utilize as part of his routine cultural speeches. Even he recognized the immense power of Albanian oral and literal tradition:

> You cannot write about the history of the Albanian people, without recognizing, without following, without discovering and studying its folklore, which mirrors the dialectic developments of that history. All events of the history of our people throughout the centuries, during the war periods, during our struggles, our joys, and sorrows have been absorbed generation after generation in the popular folklore. (Haxhihasani, 5)

The problem was that he and his regime never made any serious attempt to make the treasury of Albanian folklore available to the scholars of the outside world.

During my research for this introduction I found another major politician who had been greatly interested in the art of epic poetry. It was Harlan Berkley Peabody (1929–2009), a Harvard University graduate in Comparative Literature who had studied the oral tradition with Professor Albert B. Lord and written the foreword to Dr. Robert Elsie's *Songs of the Frontier Warriors*. He shares with us part of his experience relative to our topic:

152

I remember Lord telling me how Marshal Tito, with good intentions, instituted festival competitions to reward the best traditional singers. The judges sat with texts before them evaluating performances like the judges in *Die Meistersinger*. Singers quickly learned that to win the prize they needed to memorize an authorized text and perform it in grand style. Those who did so came out best. Few singers kept to their traditional ways. (Elsie and Mathie-Heck, vii).

If the former absolute leaders of two different countries (Albania and the former Yugoslavia) had such high consideration for the same folk poetry, I asked myself, how is it possible that their countries were such extreme enemies? As it turns out, they liked epic poetry because the people whom they represented loved their folk songs, and those songs could be used to divide as well as unite. As Zef Leka noticed, "they used epic songs to manipulate people into their political games." The Albanian epic poet Gjergj Fishta had told them long ago: "Whoever is a man of pen and letters, and is capable of comprehending in his own mind the Fatherland idea, should be able to truly understand the immense importance that the collection of folklore in itself holds for his country" (Kanuni shqip, Fishta, v). Both Hoxha and Tito must have been aware of the true power of the beautiful oral folk songs their countries had produced throughout history. I do need to do more research on Tito's use of this art, but I know firsthand that Hoxha executed and imprisoned many poets just because he was afraid that their pen would interfere with his totalitarian politics. And on top of that he denied his people access to the beautiful Slavic epic poetry. Through poetic art, people can recognize the good, the pride, the expectations, the sacrifices, and above all the true spirit of the identity of their neighbors.

The government-controlled media in Albania had made it so dramatically clear that all Montenegrins and Serbs behaved in inhuman ways toward the Albanian people, that when I was forced to flee Albania (because of my one published antigovernment poem called "Horses"), I feared that I would be subject to the same or worse punishment in Montenegro and Serbia that I had fled in Albania. Nothing could have been further from the truth. But if I had not had that experience, I would not have personally come to know Serbians like Peter Jeliç and his family, who treated me like their own son. Yet the sons of the same people killed and were killed fighting some of the bloodiest battles in Bosnia and Kosovo where half of my people live. The nature of fighting is indeed complicated in the Balkans: "Just because we kill each other doesn't mean we hate each other" I was told by Fatime Çehrja, an elderly woman from Reçi. Interestingly enough, this was the same thing a Serbian woman from Vraka had told Edith Durham in 1908: "The Moslems have killed a great many of us, but, thanks to God, we have shot plenty of them" (Durham, 17). And that is not because the loss of life has no meaning in Malësia e Madhe and Northern Albania, because it truly does:

> One song was of a widow who had two sons. The elder went to the mountain and turned robber. His mother believed him dead. The younger stayed with her, but having to cross the mountains for business was shot at from behind a rock and mortally wounded. As he lay dying the two brothers recognized one another. Horrified, the elder was about to shoot himself, when the younger cried, "Do not kill both our mother's sons. Go to her and tell her I have gone to a far country, and that you will stay with her." He died, and the robber returned home. (Durham, 48–49).

Only life without honor has no meaning. Nevertheless, the definition of honor changes from country to country in the Balkan states. How can one know if all paths that could lead to knowing each other's culture are blocked? Or even worse when the definition of honor is subject to change in accordance with the diplomacy of each other's respective political leaders? But "perhaps this struggle is the most interesting thing here, the fierce combat between two completely different elements of the human environment — the artistic dream on the one hand and the brutality of history on the other" (Zagajewski, xv).

Certainly, hatred related to territorial issues has continuously resulted in death throughout Albanian history. But this and other social and political issues mentioned above have never been limited to dealings with the neighboring countries. What we now consider minor things — ownership of a patch of land, an offending word, even over-ebullient, in-your-face celebration — have traditionally translated into fatal casualties in the northern Albanian tribes and sometimes within the families of Malësia e Madhe. But that by no means was due to hatred as we know it today. Epic poets and performers are a good example. According to author and historian Prenk Gruda (1924–1999), the mountaineers of Malësia e Madhe are among very few people in the world who for centuries have honored lahutarët (the lute players) and epic poets by holding contests where all the Balkan states at one time or another have attended. Malësia e Madhe, to the best of my knowledge, is the only place in the world that would honor the winners by naming or renaming their mountains and valleys after them:

> that is how Malësia has names of places like Vukpalaj, which until the last decade of the nineteenth century was called "Vorri i Papës." The elderly (pleqtë) would not agree if the first place

155

should go to a performer from Kosovo by the name of Qemal Palaj or the Serbian performer Dragan Vuković, who was the first cousin of the Montenegrin writer Vojvoda Gavro Vuković [Војвода Гавро Вуковић] (1852–1928). Since no woman had the nerve to stay around for that long to break the tie, they were forced to share the first prize honoring both of them. That's how we have now the compound name Vukpalaj. Vuk in short for Vuković and Palaj (Gruda, 17).

That generosity is well embedded in all three major branches of Albanian oral verse.

THE EPIC MUSE

Those three branches can be categorized as the historic epic, the songs of the Kreshniks, and the songs of the folk. The historic epic (epika historike), depending on the setting of the compositions, is also recognized by a variety of alternative names such as këngë historike (historic songs), këngë trimërie (courage songs), këngë bjeshkësh (highland songs), këngë lahute (lute songs), lirika popullore (country lyrics), and këngë burrnie (songs of virility – in the sense of virtue or nobility).

> Scholars are still uncertain at what point precisely the songs of Kosovo began to be sung. The decasyllabic poems emerging from a patriarchal village context were preceded by, and evidently for a while developed parallel to, the poems in lines of fourteen to sixteen syllables emerging from a feudal context in an urban Adriatic setting known as bugarstice. (Matthias, Vuckovici, 9)

As an integral part of the Albanian oral and literary tradition,

156

the historic epic songs have created a cultural foundation which from century to century has translated into a significant source and trusted guide in the work of upholding that much-challenged Albanian national identity. Recording the historic events, costumes, and mores of the people with maximum accuracy, these songs were regarded as potent spells that go beyond the habitual mission of telling a story. The artistic expectations of the songs are parallel with those of the heroes they portray — those who often go beyond the mere fighting of battles, fighting with a sense of personal dignity and national honor. "Word Spreads in Istanbul" is one of many songs in this category:

> Noc Mark Deda with this call
> Curdles the peace of Istanbul:
> "I'll not give up my guns alive,
> My guns I'll not give up alive!
> I'll wash the dales in blood that day
> They come to take my guns away."
> Young man with a double chin
> Noc Mark's house would enter in;
> His land's bony, the night is dark,
> They beat the door of good Noc Mark.
> Three deputies and one gendarme
> Bellow at the sleeping farm:
> "Noc Mark Deda, step outside,
> Let's see your actions match your pride!
> Orders our commandant gave:
> Bring you in dead or alive."
> "Give me five minutes more to sleep:
> Tonight a holy night I keep."
> Holy nights can swiftly pass:

157

> Noc escapes, hides in his grass.
> "God and St. Nicholas, may I
> Survive their rage and see them die:
> For my father I don't fear,
> He is in his ninetieth year
> And his time has come to die.
> I'll avenge him — if not I,
> Then my son or his son's son,
> Till we've cut ten heads for one."

Yet the fundamental mission of the historic epic songs is even greater. To simply record the essential parts of people's historic wars, social events, family activities, personal achievements, and so on is not enough; they must be recorded and performed with the highest possible literary and artistic conduct. They are real songs that deal with historical events and real people. As such, the historic epic is oriented to deal with all the intense historical, political, and social issues, even when they escalate from local to national and, at times, to international levels of conflict. Albanian historic epic songs, even when they lack specific historic data, have a poetic depth that gives the audience or reader sufficient clues to arrive at educated conclusions.

Concrete in description and realistic in interpretation, the historic songs generally do not tamper with historic outcomes regardless of how they might affect the interests of the parties involved in the conflict or how the poet might feel personally about the whole ordeal under consideration. So it is not uncommon for the poets to include details about the date and time of a social or political event or the names and the ranks of the heroes involved in a battle, leaving it to the tone and other oral and literary devices to portray the nature of the excitement resulting based on the specific outcomes. "Kole's Peerless

Women," for instance, is full of such details. In the first stanza (below), the reader is introduced to the perceived character of Gjin Nika, the nature of actions, the name of the victim, and more:

> Mountain-man, young Gjin Ndreca,
> Long had been a troublemaker.
> Now he raided Kolë Marku,
> Broke the gate of Kolë Marku,
> Broke into his sheepfold seeking
> Anything thought worth his taking:
> Copper sheep-bells from the rams,
> Tender lambs beneath their dams,
> Oxen from the manger's side,
> Kole's son's new-wedded bride.

This sense of historical fact evaluated silently by a discerning judge holds true not only for the Albanian historic epic but for its Slavic neighbors as well. They "are characterized by high sensitivity, artistic flair, concern for the meaning of man's existence on earth despite the poet's pronounced aloofness, by the strong musicality of his verses, and, above all, by consummate craftsmanship" (Dučič, x).

SONGS OF THE KRESHNIKS

Another genre in the oral literature of Albania is to be found in the songs of the Kreshniks (këngë Kreshnikës), of special importance to the inhabitants of the Malësia e Madhe. They "mirror the image of a magnificent artistic monument that speaks for the history of our people—the physiology, the ethics, the life; cautious as hasty, peaceful and gracious as combative and stubborn of our mountaineers" (Sako and Haxhihasani, 6). The Kreshniks, the heroes in this verse category, were envisioned by the poets, performers, and by their general audience as giant men of extraordinary physical power and fairytale capabilities who selflessly undertook heroic actions to protect their people and their land:

> The daughter of the King had been betrothed
> In marriage to our Gjeto-basho Muji.
> He's picked out thirty men to greet the King
> And bring the bride in triumph to her wedding.
> Sokol Halili was their chosen leader.
> But Muji held them back and said these words.
> "In God's name who created you, mark well:
> Do not dismount while you pass through the mountains,
> Do not allow your horses loose to play;
> No one should dance, though it be customary;
> You are forbidden to fire off your guns.
> For mountain-witches live about the passes,
> Whose magic can turn man and horse to stone."
> And so the wedding-guests mount to their saddles
> And set off on their journey to the King.
>
> They passed safe through the mountains of the witches,
> Remembering that they were not to dance
> Nor loose the horses on the grass to play,
> And draw back on their bridles as he told them;
> And not one shot they fired at rock or tree,
> And safe and sound they came then to the King.

These lines, taken from "Muji and the Three Witches," are

160

characteristic of the Kreshnik songs. Though such songs often deal with historic or semi-historical figures like Muji, they are often fanciful, magical, and perhaps by implication fictional in nature. Their origins are obscure. Unlike most Albanian scholars who think that "the home of the heroes, Jutbin, has been identified with the town of Udbina on the Lika River in western Croatia, about 50 km northeast of Zadar, or alternatively with the village of Udbina on the Drinjaca River in eastern Bosnia" (Elsie, 182–83), the people of Malësia e Madhe believe the home of their heroes is not Udbina in Croatia, but Gubina, a rough mountain area located between the villages Lukaj and Jugomir near Mount Veleçik.

Locals do not agree that the name "Kreshnik" is a supernatural name either. They believe the correct spelling is not "Këngët e Kreshnikëve të Utbinës," but "Katkat e Kreshtnikve të Gubinës." "The Zanas (the mountain fairies) of our mountains have turned the cave of Gubina into a permanent freshwater well so our Kreshtniks who lived forever in our Kreshta (the rockiest tip of a mountain range) would survive; the same Zanas who turned Muji and Halili from poor shepherds to Kreshtnik heroes," Prof. Llesh Rushaj of Bajza told me during a personal interview about the Albanian legendary songs. He, like many others in that area, believes that these songs are simply the songs that their sons sang while tending their animals at the very tip of the mountain range of Veleçiku, inspired by its rugged, powerful, and intimidating nature that is in accord with the very nature of the mountaineers of Malësia e Madhe.

In terms of definition, however, they agree with Robert Elsie, who claims that the Kreshnik songs "still sung by old men playing their one-stringed lahutas and two-stringed çiftelis not only in Albania but also in southern Bosnia, Montenegro, Serbia, and Kosova, are the literary reflections of legends

161

portraying and glorifying the heroic feats of warriors of the past" (Elsie, 182). They also agree that the people of Malësia e Madhe have survived "in these mountains with small patches of workable land which produce less corn than there is hunger" (Plaushaj, 20) by gaining strength from the very honor and glory traditionally illuminated in their epic songs and other artistic traditions. They love their legendary epic poems not only because are quite unique in comparison to other poetic forms, but also because they are "full of myths like orë, zana, devils, dragons, saints, and kulshedra that often fight on behalf of or against humans and other live forms on the mountains" (Hasanaj, 7). They adore them because Muji, Halili, and their people represent to the core the people of Malësia e Madhe. Just like their Kreshniks over four centuries ago, still their "stone houses are good and large — some great one-roomed structures, others with stable below and dwelling-room above" (Durham, 16). And, even though "quite unfurnished within" they still are "very fairly clean," and the children are still "bonny and newly washed." And just as their Kreshniks used to do, most of the people still manage to get "a cross tattooed on the back of the right hand" (Durham, 14).

EPIC STORY AND EPIC CYCLE

Albanian epic as a whole does not consist of long epics like Homer's Iliad and Odyssey, Virgil's Aeneid, or like the Battle of Kosovo. "The long songs are about 1,000 lines long, but the usual range is no more than 200 lines. Performers usually have about 40 to 50 songs in their individual repertoires" (Sako and Haxhihasani, 12). That is how epic poetry in the Albanian tradition is: what we might call an epic cycle or a proto-epic.

It is not a single epic poem. Because of the oppression by the Ottomans, Greeks, Romans, Slavs, and communists, among others, the Albanian epic cycle never got a chance to mature into a single coherent literary epic. But what we had was an epic tradition that was almost ripe to give birth to great epic but was always frustrated before it did so. And this is not a typically Albanian phenomenon. The Hawaiian Islands population, for instance, was great enough, its civilization was high enough, and the mythological material was rich enough for an epic to be fully composed. All they needed was for Kamehameha I (1758–1819) to stay in power long enough to create a literary tradition, and probably within a century they would have come up with a great epic about Pelé. Because the English and then the Americans took over, they have yet to make it happen.

One of the major differences between the Albanian epic and other epics is that the other epics, in a manner of speaking, created a straight line of tradition, whereas the Albanian epic developed in many small cycles, resulting in a circle of story cycles. The other traditional epics developed with plots following long straight lines with a beginning, middle, and end. Albanian poems go in small circles, creating a unique poetic tension within the larger poetic cycle. Similar symptoms have been detected by the scholars in historically much stronger countries than Albania. Take Russia as an example: "There were signs that heroic poetry was ailing and had begun to suffer from a hardening of the arteries. The first symptom of such decay is that a poet's repertory shrinks. Stories, which were once common and popular, pass out of currency, are forgotten, and no longer sung" (Bowra, 562). Fortunately the last part of Bowra's claim did not happen in the case of the Albanian epic. But the rest of his statement did. That is also because the Albanians had neither a Troy nor a Homer, neither a Rome nor a Virgil, neither an Achilles nor an Aeneas. So the epic went in circles, getting richer and stronger, to the point that the poetic cycles became like overloaded poetic domes and could no longer hold their own in the traditional form. And during the first decades of the twentieth century they naturally erupted, giving birth first to the Albanian national poet Gjergj Fishta (1871–1940), an Albanian Franciscan priest and translator, and then to Albania's only fully matured epic poem, Fishta's *The Lute of Malësia* (Lahuta e Malëcis).

It is not inconceivable that if (before the Fishta era) the Albanians had had another 100 years or so of political and economic coherence where they were not dominated by other cultures, Muji and Halili would be like other major heroes such as Achilles, Beowulf, Sigurd, Jim Cade, Karna, Roland, Siegfried, Son Wukong, and so on. In the total absence of the necessary political and economic coherence, until Fishta came into the picture, Albanian epic had no choice but to accept the fate of remaining "in the shadow of the Serbo-Croatian, or more properly, Bosnian epic, with which it has undeniable affinities" (Elsie and Mathie-Heck, xi).

The fact that art cannot be oppressed or buried forever has long been the only hope of the Albanian people, who never stopped creating and performing epic and folkloric poems. Nevertheless, they must be happy that Fishta came along. It could have been worse. According to Frederick Turner, translator of this book, there is an analogy in England: the canonical epic of King Arthur never actually existed and the closest we get is Sir Thomas Malory's *Le Morte Darthur* as printed by William Caxton. What Malory did was to amass all the Arthurian stories he could find into a fine prose collection of great Arthurian stories, but it does not quite constitute the Arthurian Epic. Why? Because the Normans invaded England.

So England archived that material, then eventually when the big flowering did happen with Shakespeare, Milton, and Spenser, the material was there for them to use. The Trojan story was oppressed for 400 years until Homer put all the stories together and collected them into a great epic. It is not that nations create languages, but rather that languages create nations (Turner).

FOLK SONG: A DIRGE IN ILLYRIA

In the Albanian oral tradition folk songs can be seen as a separate poetic genre, independent of historic and legendary epic verse. Folk songs, known in Albanian as Këngë folklorike, are subject to constant change in style, form, and subject matter. They only include and never exclude what people create and perform anywhere the Albanian language is spoken, from simple love songs, wedding songs, and healing incantations to more complex compositions such as the lament.

In Malësia e Madhe there are several recognized dirge singers. The lament is an important part of Albanian folkloric poetry. Funerary rituals are about the oldest manifestations of the human presence on this planet, but the Albanian style of lamentation is uniquely Albanian and extremely ancient. To the people of Malësia e Madhe, it gives a sense of identity to the Albanian people and their culture. It guides almost every step of a funeral ceremony. The central art of this tradition is an extemporaneous creation and delivery of verse performed by guest poets during a funeral. It is part of the last honors the mountaineers of Albania offer to their departed family members. Usually the deceased lies in a coffin with the top half of the coffin lid open. He or she is dressed in the best traditional clothes the family can afford, and those who are Christians hold a rosary in their crossed hands. As the visitors usually arrive in the hundreds and sometimes thousands to pay their last respects to the deceased and the family, they start shaking hands with the immediate family of the deceased, starting with the closest relative and continuing to greet even distant family members. The typical words they murmur are "May God give strength to you," or "May God save the rest of your loved ones," or "May God keep him in Heaven." As they accept visitors' condolences, the hosts are usually divided into two groups, men and women. Women poets are invited to lament during the ritual and each one in succession usually sits on a low stool next to the coffin. Dressed in black clothes with a white scarf on her head, each woman poet extends a larger black veil over her face in a tented manner to conceal her face. She now begins her delivery of the epic verse. She begins with an audible sigh, "HEIA," three times over. Then, with the delivery of each line of verse, she and the other female mourners simultaneously bow their veiled heads. Dirge singers alternate in their delivery of impromptu verses.

Since the legendary Albanian epic verse is concentrated mostly in the Malësia e Madhe region, I offer the reader one of the laments for the renowned Prenk Gruda (1912–1999). His funeral ceremony, at which I was present, took place in his homeland in the Montenegrin part of Malësia e Madhe. Prenk Gruda was a very well known, respected, and loved son of that region; he was a writer, schoolteacher, and a published historian who shared his life with his own birthplace of Gruda in Montenegro. As a young man, he spent most of his early adult life studying and teaching Albanian history in central Albania, mainly in the city of Elbasan. In the last part of his life he was an immigrant businessman in Michigan and Florida in the United States. Then, based on his last request to his beloved wife, Ana Gruda, a Croatian-born nurse, he was transported and buried in his beloved birthplace. I focused on his funeral not only as an ethnographic case study, but more importantly, as background to this genre of Albanian oral verse.

With this in mind, I studied six different lamenters known locally as epic poets (vajtarë / vajtare), three women and three men. I recorded their body language, their delivery style, the content of their epic verse, and the literary mechanisms they used — such as the timing of the lines, their rhythm, the use of metaphors and similes, their end rhymes, alliteration, and assonance.

Each dirge poet creates an average of 145 to 150 lines for each lamentation session, taking fourteen to fifteen minutes, which gives approximately 5 - 6 seconds, divided between the line on one hand and the long cries at the beginning and end of each line on the other. Women poets use a soft melancholic tone of voice, a monotone melody emphasizing an extended cry ("Oooo") before each line and ending each stanza with the single sad cry of "Heia." Their lines do keep an irregular A/A rhyme scheme in their couplets, with an occasional use of half rhymes. Metaphors, similes, epithets, and personifications of natural objects are incorporated into their stanzas. In terms of content, women lamenters like to concentrate on the female view of what a good person is. All three, with variations only in the chronology of their topics, emphasized in their lines Gruda's qualities as a man who sadly had to leave his country even while recognizing the good cause of his need to teach in Albania, the respect and love he always showed toward his wife and his family, his effort to keep the honor of his birthplace alive wherever he went, his charity for people in need, and the support he offered to his countrymen when they arrived in America with or without his assistance through the immigration channels:

Every child that God gives here,
When he's reached his thirteenth year,
Left his crib, and learned to speak,
Then his father he will seek,
Asks permission if he may
Into exile pass away.
Friendless in the world he'd roam:
With Preng Gruda found a home,
Food, and fire, and honor found,
Someone in a far cold land
Who could hear their voice and tongue,
Homesick, struggling, and young.
No-one, Preng, you turned away,
All who knocked your door could stay,
You would never hide nor shun,
But were friend to everyone.
HEIA

The poets often switch attention to one of the closest relatives of the deceased, vocalizing what they might imagine to be possible answers to the questions in his or her thoughts and feelings with respect to family, friends, and country on the occasion of the dear one's departure from life. They then turn their attention to the second- and third-closest relatives, emphasizing the sadness that others might feel about their loss. This would include a direct name from the immediate family or friends. Unlike the male mourners, they stay away from any criticism either of the deceased or of the people who survive him. Social qualities such as bravery, keeping one's word, the importance of receiving and giving education, and a summary of Gruda's personal achievements were part of the content.

One of the most interesting positions that lamenters took was the judging of what was sad and problematic for Gruda, not based on what the deceased personally felt was problematic, but based on the fundamental beliefs of the society from which the lamenting poet came. For example, all six lamenters who performed considered the fact that Gruda had no children as the saddest and most tragic thing that had happened apart from his own death. All this was in complete contrast with Gruda's own feelings on the issue. In a self-made recording in Detroit on June 23, 1971, which was later published on Robert Elsie's website under the section on Albanian Language and Dialect, Gruda claimed in his own voice:

> Many people feel bad because they cannot have children. I am one myself who has none. Why? It is important to help this world progress — and to simply add to the number of people on this earth, what are these people good for on earth if they do not leave works and good deeds behind? And if they don't have good intentions in life, what value do they have if they have no other purpose in life than to be like herds of animals? (Gruda)

As the lamenters performed these lines of sadness, all the other women who usually sat around the lamenting women raised their own voices chanting as a choir in support of their comments.

Following the performance of the lamenting women poets came the men. Male poet lamenters were accompanied by a Gruda family member. Depending on the space, they remained about 20 feet from the coffin. They were dressed in black business or casual suits and white shirts; a tie was optional since the ceremony was truly based on the epic tradition reaching back to when there were no ties. All three male poets took their respective turns and stood up straight with their hands on their hips, maintaining a distant facial expression. They started their laments with the highest possible tone of voice in a frightening scream-like fashion with the words "I suffer with misery because of your death, Prenk Gruda!" They averaged a time frame of 4.22 seconds per line. In terms of line meter and poetic structure their verse was just like that of the lamenting women, but the long emphasis on key words of each line increased the average time over that of each line when performed by the women lamenters. The only major difference in poetic devices and structure between the women and men was that the tone of voice passed from a normal sense of sadness into an extremely terrifying sense of loss. The other difference was the content of the subject matter. The men put more emphasis on Gruda's masculine qualities. Another major difference is that men lament only men. They do not lament women, though there are rare exceptions, whereas women lament both women and men. Although they shared the same concern for his lack of offspring as the women poets, the men considered it less tragic since he left behind many nephews and nieces, and above all he left a good name in the history of Albanian literature, nationalism, and patriotism. In their view, his numerous published books were considered an effective substitute for his lack of children. Like the women poets, they emphasized not the fact that he failed to continue his bloodline with a child, but rather that he had no son. None of the lamenters treated his love for his wife and for the other female members of his surviving family as being less important than his love for the male members of his family. Another major distinction between the men and women lamenters was that the men commented on sensitive issues concerning Gruda. They mentioned the fact that two people (Marash Mark Elezi and Marash Dojani from Hoti of Malesia e Madhe) suffered ten years of political imprisonment in the communists' toughest prisons in Albania for saving Gruda's life in his youth. The women brought up positive deeds such Gruda's helping people who wanted to immigrate to America, while the men lamenters saw this as a drain of manhood from Albanian society.

The men also started and finished their lamentation not with a cry of "Heia," as did the women, but with a screaming sound "emptying of the chest" — "EEEEH," three times over.

FOLK SONG: A WEDDING IN DAJÇ

Wedding songs are as important to Albanians as their laments. I will concentrate on a specific wedding that took place in Albania while I was conducting research for this book. This was a relevant topic because the poetry of such celebrations represents the folkloric part of Albanian epic poetry, which, in contrast to the historical epic, is not so formalized as a genre. The wedding theme is not limited to any kind of fixed subject matter. It is limitless, as it can deal with all kinds of life issues such as love, nature, the dairy, shepherds, and marriage, and includes songs of joy, victory, humor, loss, and satire, among others. Although folklore is typical throughout Albania, the historical and legendary epic is an art specific to Malësia e Madhe. The wedding is the only ceremony in Albanian culture where any other culture can be included and considered as entertainment, softening the traditional processions.

I was fortunate to find a wedding where the family and organizers were willing to let me record and take notes of their event. I am grateful to the Mikel Pjetri family of Dajç, who gave me full access to every part of their son Kol's wedding. It exemplified this very unique ceremony where tradition reigned throughout and every part of the celebration was performed in songs associated with them.

All conversations were expressed in sung verse. Religious songs, fundamentally Christian songs, followed the wedding proceedings. One night before the wedding took place, the father of the groom invited all of his immediate family to gather in his two-story home right after the performance of the Christian songs that are believed to bring good fortune to the newly married couple. He gathered his immediate family to assign the duties for the wedding day. For each duty, such as appointing individuals to deliver invitations in the villages, songs were sung as they chose the topics or duties to be discussed. The performers, the immediate family, and the hosts were dressed in traditional folk costume during this event. While the performers stood in the background, the host sat next to the fireplace, kneeling on one knee, while his wife stood behind him and the rest of the people sat in a squatting position on a rug awaiting their assignments. The families of both the bride and groom had to perform each function by combining it with the appropriate song. The family of the bride, usually the mother and a professional bride dresser, were to prepare the bride. Other members of the family, dressed in traditional costume, were showing the most important garments and jewelry that the bride was to take with her to her new home. As they showed each piece, the performers sang lines that were directly related to that garment or piece of jewelry.

> The bride is asking for a golden coin vest
> We couldn't find a golden coin vest
> And the mother said, "I will send her mine," etc.

When the bride was ready and the horse-drawn bridal

escort arrived, a song was performed announcing the escort's arrival and asking if the bride was ready. They brought one horse, which was white and especially decorated to carry the bride; a performer led a song especially for the horse. In the meantime, the performers inside the bride's room sang a song telling the bride that it was time for her to move on from being a girl to being a bride and to leave the family. Another group of ladies responded in a dialog style on behalf of the bride who was dressing and had a tear in her eyes. The lyrics expressed the sadness of the bride having to turn her back on her mother. The bride was finally dressed in her traditional costume and red facial veil. She again hears the bridal escort calling her:

> "Are you ready, our bride?
> We have come to get you.
> Stand up and embrace your father.
> Stand up and embrace your mother.
> Stand up and embrace your family . . . ."

While her father and mother accompanied her on either side, she continued to cry in a sad voice for her departure from her family. They escorted her to the horse and mounted her on the saddle. As the escort traveled with the bride, they were all singing relationship songs. When they approached the groom's home, the men and women began their folk dances announcing the arrival of the bride. The groom's whole family came to meet and greet the bride. As she descended from the horse with her face still covered with the veil, two women from the groom's family escorted her to her new bedroom. While they were dancing, they sang songs saying how lucky she was to be marrying the man she had chosen and loves; how lucky she was to come to this good house; how lucky she was that her groom had never been married; and how lucky she was to come to a house where she would always be loved and respected.

While the bride went to her room, the organizers put all kinds of rugs in the front yard and set *sofras* in the house. The father of the groom invited the family and guests to sit at the various *sofras* divided by region, gender, age, and social status. At this time, seating songs were sung. Also, a song was performed joining the two families. Men and women sang different songs depending on their interests. Most of the time they began with the line, "What a joy have we found here," immediately followed by songs to the Rakia (local spirit) which, together with the guests, was actually being served with traditional foods, including lamb and goat roasted on open spits. After the Rakia and guests had been served, other songs were heard including those containing humor and sarcasm.

The guests sat in two separate groups, and a woman performer got up from the women's section and began to sing addressing the host. She called the host a fool for inviting them for only one day because under his hospitality, they wanted to stay a week. Staying for a day, under these joyful circumstances, would only allow them to get their clothes dirty. Then the men responded, led by one man calling them bohemian women, lewdly dressed and rude. Then a young group of men joined in, siding with the women. The older men again said, "You all look like head lice and sissies." The younger men responded, "We are all handsome men; you all are fart faces." Then the young men and the women closed the comic contest by telling the old men, "May you all go bald." Next from the various guests came all kinds of nature songs, love songs, and bravery songs; and these preceded the professional entertainment of a group with a band. Then the bride came out and presented herself to the guests. Her father uncovered her face and everyone began singing songs about the specific features of the bride's beauty. They sang the traditional lines, "How beautiful is our bride / Marshalla, Marshalla." They compared her eyes to coffee cups. They compared her body's grace to that of a cypress tree, her face was sweet as cookies, and her brows were like the crescent of the moon. Her mouth was that of a small jewelry box. All of that was followed by a final couplet wishing a good life together for the bride and groom, and hopes that they would multiply like the seed on the ground and grow together like a cotton tree.

The closing song was performed while everyone was dancing by a single performer who sang a song addressed to the cities in other regions, asking them "Why do you look at us strangely . . . just because I don't want your girls? The girls of Dajç are kind to me and they are willing to dance with me."

ORAL POETRY AS GIFT

As I interviewed poets, epic singers, and ordinary people in Malësia e Madhe, I recognized something that might turn into a lifelong project for me. The people of this area like to keep some songs to themselves, worrying that they be might stolen or plagiarized. It all started with a conversation I had with Marash Marku, a well-informed 84-year-old man, who never had any formal education. After I introduced myself and explained my mission to him, he was hesitant to engage in further conversation. He asked my name again, and nothing happened.

"Who did you say you are working with, again?" he asked.

"With the American poet and professor Frederick Turner," I replied.

"Ah, I know who he is, another Alfred Lord . . . ." He sounded disappointed.

"What do you know about him?"

Said he, "I do not like what he said about beauty. According to our pumpkin-head news announcers he sees beauty as embarrassing as rasha e grave (a womans' dress)."

Only after I reframed Turner's quote as best I could—which in its correct version is:

> The word beauty is a little embarrassing; there is something old-fashioned about it, like a country girl wearing her mother's dress. It is precisely for this reason that I shall use it rather than the much cooler and more stylish term the aesthetic. The aesthetic is often either a euphemism for that coarse and lachrymose old beauty or a hard, free, clean and cruel substitute for it, steel flowers for the bride. (Turner, 1)

—did he start to talk. For reasons that he preferred to keep to himself, I felt his disappointment with the American scholar Alfred Lord. Later, however, he explained to me the reasons for his hesitation and promised to tell me about a unique song that "no one knows," according to him. Here are his exact words:

> There are some honest epic poetry collectors in the world. Some are not. They go about acting as if they are singing to their lutes, and slowly but surely steal someone's work or just mimic somebody else's songs. But if you want to tell me that there is nothing new in Albanian epic poetry, I would advise you to think again. We save our songs better than our money, even though we have more songs than money. Some time ago I heard a new lute song. There was absolutely nothing new in it and it was based upon the motive in the Malësia e Madhe. It was almost absolute theft. I know a man who writes folkloric songs by taking to pieces

the work of someone else and putting it together in his own way, changing a few names of people and places — and there you go, he calls it an epic poem of his own country. His song is as lifeless and as cheap as his character is.

What I got from Marku made me think for a long time. The first thought that crossed my mind had to do with the fact that there must be a lot more epic songs that no one knows about. The conversation with him confirmed my earlier feeling that translators have to make as great a submission of identity as the people who are being translated. In other words, they treat poetry as a very valuable gift. In those terms, for them gift-giving is absolutely fundamental to their culture; it is a matter of honor, a matter of hospitality, and their way of life. Their incredible care for the art of epic poetry makes you feel that you are translating their identity, their very soul; it makes you feel that you are the recipient of a great gift or a great honor. In a way, as translators, Turner and I were like strangers who came to them like Odysseus coming to the island of Phaiakia to receive the greatest gift, one that represents a symbolic rebirth for Odysseus. And we as translators can only repay them by giving them away to the rest of the world, so that the rest of the world may recognize the greatness of the gift their culture has given.

Impressed as I was with Marku's epic diatribe, I tried to recall things I had read in the past about how the mountaineers of Malësia e Madhe felt about sharing their ideas with their Slavic neighbors. Serbian by nationality, Petar II Petrović-Njegoš (1813–1851), a poet who is also considered the national poet of Montenegro, came to mind. He was known for borrowing popular ideas and reproducing out of them peerless epic poems such as those included in his book *The Mountain Wreath*

(Kundora e Maleve. Serb. Горски вијенац or Gorski vijenac). Only after recognizing the similarities in poetic expression, form, philosophical approach, and other important features between Njegoš' work and the Albanian epic, did I start to understand why Marku hesitated to "hand" me his "secret" poems. I also saw why Njegoš' translators from Serbian into Albanian had downplayed the tension of an ongoing argument at that time by making this statement in their introduction to *The Mountain Wreath*: "it is natural that two neighbors borrow from each other the flour for their daily bread, and even more so when it comes to their thoughts, feelings, and rituals" (Mekuli and Nekaj, xix).

Despite the fact that Njegoš' translators had conceded that "without question, Njegoš' has taken these songs from the mouth of the people and has reprocessed them" (Nokshiqi, xviii), Marku was not satisfied. Though a man of his honorable caliber would not make direct accusations about Njegoš, Marku must have felt that a poem is a gift only when it is given to you, not when it is taken from you. On the other hand, as Nuhi Vinca argues, "Poets do not belong to a particular people but to the whole of humanity, but to be the poets of the words they must first be poets of their own people" (Vinca, 198). Frasheri went even further, saying that:

> Although it was created by an individual artist, the folk song is the property of all, rather than the property of its originator. This may have happened in the following manner: An event of importance took place in the region (let us say, a fight between two brave warriors, and so on); and quickly the unknown poet, in order to sanctify the event, composed a song, which he then perhaps sang to his fellow villagers in an open field, or perhaps in the church courtyard. Having won the hearts of everybody,

the song spread from person to person, and finally became the property of the people. In time, the name of its creator was forgotten, and each subsequent singer added, subtracted, or changed parts of the song to suit his taste. For example, I found that the Song of Zanë—a popular name in Mirditë—is also sung in Shosh in the Dukagjin region, but in a different form. (Frasheri, 88)

This is a statement that since the time of its publication has been widely used as an example by both those who agree with Frasheri and those who, like Zef Gjergji, think "he must have 'lost' his mind" when he wrote it.

The truth is, Turner and I knew all about this unique tension in the Balkan Peninsula already. Most American scholars of Albania do. But the true mission of this trip was to do primary research, interviewing the very few traditional Albanian epic poets still alive, and asking them for the most meaningful gift they could give: a few hours' pass into their epic poems and through them into their matchless hearts. And they so gracefully complied. If the poems in this collection and their openhearted interviews give the English-speaking reader a greater insight into Albania's tragic and joyful history, it is thanks to them.

WORKS CITED AND CONSULTED

Andric, Ivo. The Bridge on the Drina. Trans. Lovett F. Edwards
        Chicago: The University of Chicago Press, 1977.
Bala, Vehbi, et al. Historia e Letërsisë Shqiprare. Tirana:
        Akademia e Shkencave e RPS tëShqipërisë, 1983.
Ballhysa, Hatije and Pavli Haxhillazi, Studime
        Historike. Vols. 1-4. Tirana: Akademia e Shkencave

ERSH Instituti i Historisë, 1996.

Barleti, Marin. Rrethimi i Shkodrës. Tirana: Kombinati Poligrafik, 1982.

Biagini, Antonelo. Historia e Shqipëtarisë. Milano: Bompiani, 1998.

Bosley, Keith, ed. Poetry of Asia, Five Millenniums of Verse from Thiry-three Languages. New York: Weatherhill, 1979.

Bowra, C. M. From Virgil to Milton. London: Macmillan & Co. Ltd, 1948.

—. Heroic Poetry. New York: St Martin's Press, 1966.

Çapaliku, Alfred, Miaser Dibra and Shpresa Rama. Paralele Folklorike Ndërkufitare. Shkodër: Camaj-Pipa, 2005.

Ceadel, Eric B., ed. Literature of the East. New York: Grove Press, Inc., 1959.

Cozens-Hardy, W.H. "Montenegro and its Borderlands." The Geographical Journal 5 (1894): 385.

Dibrani, Shefqet. Virtyte e Visare. Prishtina: Faik Konica, 2010.

Dučič, Jovan. Blue Legends. Trans. Vasa D. Mihailovich Columbus: Kosovo Publishing Company, 1983.

Durham, Edith. High Albania A Victorian Traveler's Balkan Odyssey. London: Phoenix Press, 2000.

Elsie, Robert. "Thoughts on the meaning of life, Prenk Gruda (1912-1999)." n.d. Albanian Literature in Translation. 12 February 2011 <http://www.albanianlanguage. net/en/dialects/rec_map1CG.html>.

Elsie, Robert. A Dictionary of Albanian Religion, Mythology, and Folk Culture. London: Hurst & Company, 2001.

—. History of Albanian Literature. Vols. i, II. New York: Columbia University Press, 1995.

—. Tales form Old Shkodra, Early Abanian Short Stories. Ed.

Robert Elsie. Pejë: Dukagjini, 2004.

Elsie, Robert and Janice Mathie-Heck, Songs of Frontier Warriors. Trans. Robert Elsie and Janice Mathie-Heck. Wauconda: Bolchazy-Caducci Publishers, Inc., 2004.

Floqi, KR. Patriotismë e Nacionalismë. Tirana: Kristo P. Luarasi, 1928.

Frasheri, Stavre Th. Through Mirdite in Winter. Trans. Peter R. Prifti. Boulder: East European Monographs, 2002.

Friedrich, Paul. Music in Russian Poetry. New York: Peter Lang Publishing, Inc., 1998.

Gebert, Armand. "Albanians, Croatians pick Detroit." The Detroit News 21 February 1983: 4-B.

Gruda, Prenk. "Gruda: unë Jam malësor: intervistë nga Gjekë Marinaj." The Poets' Times April-May 1998: 17.

Gërcaliu, Mustafa, Qemal Haxhihasani and Jorgo Panajoti, Çeshtje të Folklorit Shqiptar. Vol. 1. Tirana: Akadeia e Shkencave e RPS të Shqipërisë, 1982.

Gjçovi, Shtjefën. Kanui i Lek Dukagjinit. Shkodër: Albinform, 1993.

Gjeçov, Shtjefën, ed. The Code of Lekë Dukagjini. Trans. Leonard Fox. New York: Gjonlekaj Publishing Company, 1989.

Grabowicz, George G. Toward a History of Ukrainian Literature. Cambridge: Harvard University Press, 1981.

Hasanaj, Gjergj. Malësori Këndon. Titograd: Cetinë, 1971.

Haxhihasani, Qemal and Miranda Dule, Epika Historike Vol. II. Tirana: Akademia e shkencave e RPS të Shqipërisë, 1981.

Haxhihasani, Qemal. Epika Historike. Vol. I. Tirana: Akademia e Shkencave e RPSSH, 1983.

—. Epika Lengjendare. Ed. Qemal Haxhihasani. Vol. II. Tirana: Akademia e Shkencave e RPS të Shqipërisë, 1983.

—. Folklor Shqiptar, Epika Legjendare. Ed. Qemal Haxhihasani. Vol. II. Tirana: Instituti i Folklorit, 1966.

—. Këngë Popullore Legjendare. Ed. Qemal Haxhihasani. Tirana: Instituti i Shkencave, 1955.

Irving, Washington. "Rip Van Winkle." Riverside Literature Series October 1891.

Karadzic, Vuk. Songs of the Serbian People. Trans. Milne Holton and Vasa D. Mihailovich. Pittsburgh: University of Pittsburgh Press, 1997.

Kramoris, Ivan J., trans. An Anthology of Slovak Poetry. Pennsylvania: The Obrana Press, Inc., 1947.

Kussi, Matti, Keith Bosley and Michael Branch, Finish Folk Poetry-Epic. Helsinki: Finish Literature Society, 1977.

Lord, Albert B. The Singer of Tales. Cambridge: Harvard University Press, 1971.

Marku, Marash. An interview with Marash Marku. Gjekë Marinaj. 30 May 2006.

Marku, Vasil. Koncert i Margimatarit. cond. Vladimir Husimi. By Maliq Herri. New York, 1994.

Matejka, Ladislav, J. Mersereau and D. Welsh, Czech Poetry A Bilingual Anthology. Vol. I. University of Michigan, 1973.

Matthias, John and Vladeta Vuckovic, The Battle of Kosovo Athens: Ohio University Press, 1987.

McNamee, Maurice B., S.J. Honor and the Epic Hero. New York: Holt, Rinehart and Winston, Inc., 1960.

Meta, Beqir. Federata Panshqiptare "Vatra" . Tirana: Globus R., 2002.

Murrin, Michael. The Allegorical Epic. Chicago and London: The University of Chicago Press, 1980.

Nuhi, Vinca. Poetika e Lirikës Popullore Shqiptare. Strugë: IRIS, 2006.

—. Poetika E Lirikës Gojore Strugane. Strugë: IRIS, 2006.

Okpewho, Isidore. The Epic in Africa, Towards a Poetics of the
     Oral Performance. New York: Columbia University
     Press, 1979.

Palushaj, Lulash N. Malsia dhe Fiset e Saj. Lezhë: Enti Botues
     Poligrafik, 1996.

Parker, Patricia A. Inescapable Romance, Studies in the Poetics
     of a Mode. Princeton: Princeton University Press, 1979.

Pavlovich, Miodrag. The Conqueror in Constantinople. Trans
     Joachim Neugroschel. New York: New Rivers Press,
     1976.

Petroviq-Njegosh, Petr. Kunora e Maleve. Prishtinë: Mustafa
     Bakija, 1952.

Pipa, Arshi. Contemporary Albanian Literature. New York:
     Eastern european Monographs, 1991.

Popa, Vasko. Earth Erect. Trans. Anne Pennington. London:
     Anvil Press Poetry, 1973.

Prifti, Peter R. Land of Albanians: A Crossroads of Pain and
     Pride. Tirana: Horizont, 2002.

Quint, David. Epic and Empire, Politics and Generic Form From
     Virgil to Milton. Princeton: Princeton University Press,
     1992.

Reeder, Roberta, ed. Russian Folk Lyrics. Trans. Roberta Reeder.
     Bloomington and Indianapolis: Indiana Universit
     Press, 1975.

Rrjolli, Fatime . An interview with Fatime Rjolli. Gjekë Marinaj.
     30 May 2006.

Rushaj, Llesh . An interview with Prof. Llesh Rushaj. Gjekë
     Marinaj. 28 May 2006.

Schaarschmidt, Gunter. Poetica Slavica:1981Studies in Honour
     of Zbigniew Folejewski. Ed. J. Douglas Clayton and
     Gunter Schaarschmidt. Ottawa: University of Ottawa

Press, 1981.

Schwandner-Sievers, Stephanie and Bernd J. Fischer, Albanian Identities Myth and History. Bloomington: Indiana University Press, 2002.

Shaw, Albert. "Who are Abanians and what do they want." The American Review of Reviews XLVII.January-June (1913): 224-236.

Shtëpia, Dedgjon. Ushtimë Lahutare. Shkodër: Shijefni, 2008.

Shuteriqi, Dimitër S. Shkrimet Shqipe në Viete 1332-1850. Prishtina: Rilindja, 1978.

Smith, Gerald S., trans. Contemporary Russian Poetry, A Bilingual Antology. Bloomington: Indiana University Press, 1993.

Spathari, Nikolla. Malësia e Madhe siç e njoha unë. Shkodër Idromeno, 2001.

Streissguth, Tom. Albania in Pictures. Visual Geographic Series, 2nd. Minneapolis: Twenty First Century Books, 2011.

Swinburne, Algernon Charles. Songs of Two Nations. London: Chatto & Windus, Piccadilly, 1893.

Tadic, Novica. Dark Things. Trans. Charles Simic. Rochester: BOE Editions, Ltd, 2009.

Turner, Frederick. Beauty: The Value of Values. Charlottesville and London: University Press of Virginia, 1991.

Ukgjini, Dom Nikë. Shkreli Vështrim Historiko-Kulturor Shkodër: At Gjergj Fishta , 1998.

Unknown. "The Royal Asiatic Society: an Appeal." The China Journal VIII.6 (1928): 288-289 (Literary Supplement Pamphlet).

Zagajewski, Adam, ed. Polish Writers on Writing. San Antonio: Trinity University Press, 2007.

Zogiani, Salih. Albanian Anecdotes. Trans. Avni Spahiu. Prishtina: Printing Press, 2006.

—. Anekdota. Vol. I and III. Prishtina: Printing Press, 2007.
    Zojsi, Rrok; Dojaka, Abaz, and Hasan Qatipi. "Arti
    Popullor në Shqipëri." Akademia e Shkencave të
    RPSh: Instituti i Historisë, Sektori i Etnografisë, 1976.
    2-Pamphlet.

THE RECORDINGS

HOMAGE TO THE WARRIORS
    was performed by Fran Zef Therçaj (1918-1996). The
    poem comes to us as a private recording by his son
    Tom Therçaj, a prominent journalist who works for the
    State Television of Albania, TVSH.

THE EAGLE OF ALBANIA
    was performed by Noc Tom Dedaj and recorded in
    Koplik, on May 26, 2006 by Gjekë Marinaj.

THE PLEDGE OF THE HILL
    was performed by Resmie Siqeca and recorded in
    Vlorë, on June 2, 2006 by Gjekë Marinaj.

IN THE MOUNTAINS OF TARAMIS
    was performed by Nik Palok Marinaj and recorded in
    Richardson, Texas, on June 11, 2008 by Gjekë Marinaj.

MY HOME VILLAGE
    was performed by Klarko Koçi and recorded in Porto
    Palermo, Vlorë, on June 2, 2006 by Gjekë Marinaj.

MILKING-TIME
    was performed by Pashko Gjekaj and recorded in
    Vukpalaj, Bajzë, on June 5, 2006 by Gjekë Marinaj.

CHEESE
    was performed by Pashko Gjekaj and recorded in
    Vukpalaj, Bajzë, on June 5, 2006 by Gjekë Marinaj.

BUTTER
    was performed by Pashko Gjekaj and recorded in

Vukpalaj, Bajzë, on June 5, 2006 by Gjekë Marinaj.

SHEPHERD'S SONG
was performed by Dakë Keqaj and recorded in Peraj,
Bajzë, on June 5, 2006 by Gjekë Marinaj.

THE PROUD ROOSTER
was performed by Zef Leka and recorded in Ndrecaj,
Bajzë, on May 29, 2006 by Gjekë Marinaj.

DEDË LUL TOMA
was performed by Gjok Gojçaj and recorded in Detroit,
Michigan, on October 25, 2008 by Gjekë Marinaj.

KOLË'S PEERLESS WOMEN
was performed by Nik Palok Marinaj and recorded in
Richardson, Texas, on June 12, 2008 by Gjekë Marinaj.

YLBER
was performed by Fran Zef Therçaj (1918-1996). The
poem comes to us as a private recording by his son
Tom Therçaj.

WORD SPREADS IN ISTANBUL
was performed by the epic poet Jonuz Delaj and
recorded in Koplik, on June 5, 2006 by Gjekë Marinaj.

ZEK JAKINI
was performed by Jaho Margjeka and recorded in
Tirana, on June 4, 2006 by Gjekë Marinaj.

SUNG ACROSS THE SHOULDER
 was performed by Pjetër Gjokë Kodra and recorded in
 Koplik, on June 4, 2006 by Gjekë Marinaj.

THE MARRIAGE OF HAJKUNA
 was performed by Nik Palok Marinaj and recorded in
 Richardson, Texas, on June 19, 2008 by Gjekë Marinaj.

MUJI AND THE THREE WITCHES
 was performed by Prof. Lesh Rushaj and recorded in
 Rome on May 23, 2006 by Gjekë Marinaj.

"SWEET, WHERE WERE YOU LINGERING?"
 was performed by Lush Vukelaj and recorded in
 Koplik on May 29, 2006 by Gjekë Marinaj.

"WHERE SHALL WE MEET?"
 was performed by Pjetër Gjokë Kodra and recorded in
 Koplik on May 29, 2006 by Gjekë Marinaj.

BEAUTY WITH A WHITE SHAWL
 was performed by Lush Vukelaj and recorded in
 Koplik on May 29, 2006 by Gjekë Marinaj.

"MILLER, MILLER"
 was performed by Pjetër Gjokë Kodra and recorded in
 Koplik on May 29, 2006 by Gjekë Marinaj.

TWO BEAUTIES
 was performed by Zef Marinaj and recorded in Koplik
 on May 30, 2006 by Gjekë Marinaj.

BEAUTY AT THE DOOR

>was performed by Prof. Lesh Rushaj and recorded in Rome on May 23, 2006 by Gjekë Marinaj.

"HEY, GIRL"

>was performed by Prof. Lesh Rushaj and recorded in Rome on May 23, 2006 by Gjekë Marinaj.

"HEY, BEAUTIFUL"

>was performed by Dakë Keqaj and recorded in Peraj, Bajzë, on Junë 3, 2006 by Gjekë Marinaj.

TO THE BRIDE

>was performed by Luxhe Gjeloshja and recorded in Koplik on May 30, 2006 by Gjekë Marinaj.

THE COCK AND THE BRIDE

>was performed by Noc Tom Dedajand recorded in Koplik on May 30, 2006 by Gjekë Marinaj.

SHE WHISPERS TO HER LOVER

>was performed by Vera Zef Kodra and recorded in Koplik on May 30, 2006 by Gjekë Marinaj.

POOR HYSEN

>was performed by Jaho Margjeka and recorded in Tirana, on June 4, 2006 by Gjekë Marinaj.

MARTA GOSSIPS

>was performed by Vera Zef Kodra and recorded in Koplik on May 30, 2006 by Gjekë Marinaj.

A CHARM AGAINST SNAKEBITE
> was performed by Zef Marinaj and recorded in Koplik
> on May 30, 2006 by Gjekë   Marinaj.

SONG OF THE SALT
> was performed by Zef Marinaj and recorded in Koplik
> on May 30, 2006 by Gjekë   Marinaj.

CURING A BUNION
> was performed by Luxhe Gjeloshja and recorded in
> Koplik on May 30, 2006 by Gjekë Marinaj.

HOST AND GUEST
> was performed by Dedë Shtëpija and recorded in New
> York on November 30, 2010 by Gjekë Marinaj.

HAT SONG
> was performed by Dedë Shtëpija and recorded in New
> York on November 30, 2010 by Gjekë Marinaj.

THE BIRTHDAY OF SAINT NICHOLAS
> was performed by Luxhe Gjeloshja and recorded in
> Koplik on May 30, 2006 by Gjekë Marinaj.

THE BLESSED VIRGIN
> was performed by Vera Zef Kodra and recorded in
> Koplik on May 30, 2006 by Gjekë Marinaj.

TO THE CHRISTIAN PRIEST)
> Dr. Miodrag Radulovacki contributed to this book
> by performing this poem passed down to him by his
> grandfather, Stevan Loš (1890-1943).

LAMENT FOR PRENG GRUDA
> was performed by one of the women lamenters who, as the tradition has it, never introduced herself.

LET YOUR WORK BE WELL OR ILL...
> was performed by Zef Leka and recorded in Ndrecaj, Bajzë, on May 29, 2006 by Gjekë Marinaj.

WHAT IS WITHIN A MAN
> was performed by Resmie Siqeca and recorded in Vlorë, on June 2, 2006 by Gjekë Marinaj.

THE ORAL POETS AND PERFORMERS

Photo courtesy of Gj. Dedaj

DEDAJ, Noc Tom

Noc Tom Dedaj is a school teacher and a supporter of epic poetry and epic poets. Born in the village of Shkrel, Albania, in 1945, Dedaj is among very few people of that background who has a University level education. He is now retired and enjoys spending time in his private studio reading.

Photo by Gjekë Marinaj

DELAJ, Januz

Born in Nikç, Kelmend, Albania, in 1950, Januz Delaj is a professional lahutar (lutenist) and a well-known epic poet in composition and performance. He has performed in numerous national (Albanian) and international folk festivals and concerts with outstanding success. Even though his twelfth grade level education is not related to music, this self-taught artist is a top ten epic performer not only in Albania but anywhere Albanian communities reside.

Photo by Gjekë Marinaj

GJEKAJ, Pashko

A cultural director and a theatrical performer, Pashko Gjekaj was born in Pjetroshan, Albania, in 1946. He made a name for himself as an arts academician who utilized his university level training to bring the artistic environment of Malësia e Madhe to a higher level. Gjekaj is regarded by his peers as an innovator who takes concrete steps toward the promotion of artistic activities and cultural reform. Epic and folk poetry have always been his passion.

199

Photo by Gjekë Marinaj

GJELOSHJA, Luxhe

Once a farmer and now a housewife, Luxhe Gjeloshja was born in Shkrel, Malësia e Madhe, in 1941. After completing her fourth grade of education, she developed an interest in epic poetry, especially religious and love songs. Although she has never performed in public, she never hesitates to recite them in private when asked to do so.

Photo courtesy of V. Gojçaj

GOJÇAJ, Gjok

Gjok Gojçaj (1914-2010) worked as a mason from his youth until his retirement. Born and raised in Skorraq-Hot, Montenegro, Gojçaj kept alive his family tradition by being honorable, brave and generous, making his home and hospitality available to all friends and neighbors, including strangers in need. Gjok was survived by his wife Djellë Gojçaj (above) and their children, who now live in Detriot, Michigan.

201

Photo courtesy of A. Keqaj

KEQAJ, Dakë

Dakë Keqaj is the author of several volumes of poetry and is widely acknowledged as one the best poets of Malësia e Madhe. He was a fan-favorite athlete in his early twenties, working for the state of Albania as a health inspector until the fall of communism in 1991. Now he enjoys his retirement; occasionally he prefers to help out the local television stations of Malësia e Madhe with their programming needs. Keqaj continues to write poetry as well.

Photo by Gjekë Marinaj

KOÇI, Klarko

Klarko Koçi was born in Qeparo, Albania, in 1944. Soon after earning his high school diploma, Koçi started working as a laborer and continued doing so until recently. Now he is a castle docent at Ali Pasha Tepelena's castle, located in Porto Palermo, Albania.

Photo by Gjekë Marinaj

KODRA, Pjeter Gjokë

When Pjeter Gjoke Kodra, a laborer, moved from Shalë-Dukagjin, Albania, where he was born in1959, to Koplik (the only city in the district of Malësia e Madhe), all he had to offer to his new neighbors was his physical strength, his eighth grade education and an enormous love for epic poetry. Yet that was all he needed to earn their respect and enjoy his own way of life in the small northern Albanian city where he lives with his wife Vera and their children.

Photo by Gjekë Marinaj

LEKA, Zef

Zef Leka was born Bajzë, Albania, in 1935. With only an eighth grade education he managed to find employment as the only Public Registrar of the entire Malësia e Madhe district, a job he loved for over 40 years. Although he never published any of his own work, Leka never lost his passion for epic poetry. His main goal in life was to support his children in getting their advanced university degrees, and he takes great pride in achieving it.

Photo by Gjekë Marinaj

MARGJEKA, Jaho

Jaho Salih Margjeka was born in Bujan, Tropojë, Albania, in 1961. He graduated from the University of Tirana, with a degree in Albanian language and literature, in 1989. Margjeka has authored several volumes of poetry and prose for which he has been honored with numerous literary awards and cultural recognitions. Margjeka is currently a senior journalist for Radio Tirana.

Photo by Gjekë Marinaj

MARINAJ, Nik Palok

Nik Palokë Marinaj, the father of Gjekë Marinaj (this book's co-translator) was born in Brrut, Malësia e Madhe, Albania, in 1939. An optimist at heart, he never complains about the extremely difficult conditions in which he raised and educated his seven children. As a lifelong farmer, whenever he would set aside his mattock and shovel he would pick up his *lahutë* or *çifteli* to entertain himself and his family. His fourth grade level of education enabled him to write down hundreds of folk and epic songs before he learned them by heart.

207

Photo by Gjekë Marinaj

MARINAJ, Zef

Zef Marinaj, whose lifelong career as warehouse director, first in Zagora and later in Koplik, made him a prominent man for helping everyone who asked for his aid with government supplies, was born in Kastrat, Albania, in 1937. Regardless of his eighth grade education, many people consider him to be a wise man not only for managing to do that without being imprisoned but also for his great talent at composing and interpreting proverbs and anecdotes. He is the most acclaimed man in Malësia e Madhe.

Photo by Gjekë Marinaj

MARKU, Marash

A humble farmer, with only a first grade level of education, Marash Marku (1926-2010) knew by heart over 500 epic songs. Born and raised in Brrut, Malësia e Madhe, Albania, Marku moved to Bajzë during his late fifties in search for a better life for his children Dilë, Llesh, Marie, Groshe, and Fran. He was a most knowledgeable person on the subject of the epic poetry of the Balkan states.

Photo courtesy of D. Palushaj

PALUSHAJ, Lulash Nikë

A published poet and historian, Lulash Nikë Palushaj was born in Bekaj, Triesh, Montenegro, in 1944. He studied college level language and literature in Prishtina. Palushaj is also known for his contributions as a dance choreographer not only in Malësia e Madhe but also in the Albanian community in Detroit, Michigan, where he now lives with his family.

Photo courtesy of Dr. M. Radulovacki

RADULOVACKI, Miodrag

The 2010 UIC Inventor of the Year, Dr. Miodrag Radulovacki, is a Professor of Medicine at the University of Illinois at Chicago. Born in Hrtkovci (Screm), Serbia, 1933, Dr. Miodrag Radulovacki contributed to this book by performing poetry passed down to him by his grandfather, Stevan Loš (1890-1943).

211

Photo courtesy of J. Rushaj

RUSHAJ, Llesh

Llesh Rushaj, born in Bajzë, Kastrat (Albania) in 1943, started teaching Albanian language and literature immediately after graduating from college at what is now called "Dodë Kaçaj" High School. While keeping up with his professional duties as a popular teacher, he spent much of his free time collecting unpublished epic songs and studying the origin and the history of their words. While still an etymologist at heart, Rushaj is now retired and lives in Italy with his wife Vitore.

212

Photo courtesy of K. Deda

SHTËPIJA, Dedë

Dedë Shtëpija was born in Xhan, Dukagjin, Shkoder in 1938. He is well-known epic poetry performer on both instruments, the lahutë and the çifteli. A retired farmer, Shtëpija has an eighth grade level education. He is the author of one book of rhapsodic poetry.

213

Photo by Gjekë Marinaj
SIQECA, Resmie

Born in Vlorë, Albania in 1920, Resmie Siqeca has survived many dramatic political changes that Albania has been through, including World War II and over four decades of communist dictatorship. She knows many religious and patriotic poems by heart and performs them beautifully. The communist regime took everything away from her, including her daughter Burbuqe and her son-in-law Dalan Luzaj, who were banished from their village and isolated in a government controlled environment. Yet, her honest soul, her love for Islam, for her family, and for her epic poetry were hidden deeper than the communists could ever dig. Considering the circumstances, she is proud of her fourth grade level of education.

214

Photo courtesy of T. Therçaj

THERÇAJ, Fran Zef

Fran Zef Therçaj (1918-1996) was born in Lukaj of Kastrat, Malësia e Madhe, Albania. He was a folk dancer and singer. His last public performance dates back to about six months before the diplomatic relations between Albania and former Federal Republic of Yugoslavia reached a virtual dead end. Before that time, he had been leading a group of folk entertainers who performed in the cities of Albania and its neighboring countries. He was much admired by the people of Malësia e Madhe. The poem comes to us as a private recording by his son Tom Therçaj, a prominent journalist who works for the State Television of Albania, TVSH.

Photo by Gjekë Marinaj

VUKELAJ, Lush

Farming was the only option Lush Gjelosh Vukelaj had to support his family. He lost favor with the communist government and suffered the consequences during his entire adult life. Only after his two sons Angjelin and Aleks managed to escape the authorities in 1990 to immigrate to America did his life gain some normalcy. Born in 1935, Gjeloshi lives in Shkrel, Albania, were he had initially earned his fourth grade education.

Photo by Gjekë Marinaj

ZEFI, Vera

Right after graduating from high school, Vera Zef Kodra started her career as a seamstress, a profession she loves and plans to keep until she decides to retire. She was born in Vukpalaj of Kastrat, in 1963, were she first started to learn by heart many of the long epic poems she knows and privately performs today.

217

INDEX

Index

221

Noel Malcolm 144
Novi Pazar 151

O

Odysseus 15, 177
Oedipus 24
Old man Kasel 102
Oral Poetry as a Gift Exchange
    135
Orthodox 10
Ottoman Sultan Murat I 139

P

Paladin 14, 101
Parry 19, 29, 151
Patriotic Songs 35
Peja 71, 149
Pelé 163
Petar II Petrović-Njegoš 178
Popol Vuh 20
Preng Gruda 123, 168, 123, 194
Prince 61, 62, 63, 64, 65, 66, 67
Proto-epic 136, 162
Pulat 144

Q

Qemal Palaj 156
Qeparo 44, 203

R

Raška dstrict 143
Renaissance 145
Robert Elsie 147, 152, 161, 169,
    181
Roland 164

Romans 30, 163
Ronsard 19
Russia 163

S

Saint Nicholas 119, 120
Sako 138, 160, 162
Salih Ugljanin 151
Salt 112
Sanjak 151
Sannazaro 19
Sarajevo 102
Scots border ballads 9
Scots-Irish heroes 19
Selim Spahiu 59
Serbia, 143, 161, 211
Serbian 29, 142, 145, 146, 154,
    156, 178, 182
Serbian scholars 142
Serbo-Croatian 151, 164
Shakespeare 19, 140, 165
Shkoder 40, 57, 71, 213
Shkrel 15, 91, 101, 143, 197,
    200, 216
Shuteriqi 139, 144, 184
Sidney 19
Sir Thomas Malory 164
Slavic, 146
Slavic origins 142
Software 22
Songs of the Dairy 12
Songs of the Serbian People
    145, 182
South Slavs 146
Spenser, 165